Starry, Starry Night

Provincetown's Response to the AIDS Epidemic

Jeanne Braham
& Pamela Peterson

Lumen Editions
a division of Brookline Books

ISBN 1-57129-058-3

Library of Congress Cataloging-In-Publication Data
Braham, Jeanne, 1940–
    Starry, starry night : Provincetown's response to the AIDS epidemic
/ Jeanne Braham & Pamela Peterson.
       p.   cm.
    ISBN 1-57129-058-3 (pbk.)
    1. AIDS (Disease)--Massachusetts--Provincetown.   I. Peterson,
Pamela (Pamela C.).   II. Title.
RA644.A25B695   1998
362.1'969792'00974492--dc21   98-4155
                                                                CIP

Book design and typography by Erica L. Schultz.

Printed in USA by Data Reproductions Corporation, Auburn Hills, MI.

10   9   8   7   6   5   4   3   2   1

Published by
Lumen Editions
a division of BROOKLINE BOOKS
P.O. Box 1047
Cambridge, Massachusetts 02238
Order toll-free: 1-800-666-BOOK

Contents

For those who live with AIDS;
for those whose voices are never recorded

Acknowledgments

This book is about a community's response to a terrible epidemic, a story honoring collective action and collective memory. Its successful completion required collaboration, not only by two authors who brought very different skills and training to the task, but also by a number of friends and colleagues who offered support, advice, and, frequently, practical help. We'd like to thank: Thomas Antonelli, Dorothy Braham, George Bryant, Chris Clifton, Anne Eberle, Jane Garrett, Diana Hume George, Ellen Harris, Tai Hazard, Deborah Hilty, Sonya Jones, Nancy Lotta, Lianne and Everett McDonald, Sue and Tom Mullen, John Quinn, Gary Reinhardt, Beth Reynders, Chris Shipley, Bea Smith, Janis Sommers, Jessica Tuffley, Jessica Tudryn, Lynn Walterick, Bev Whitbeck, Kristin Woolever, Paul Zolbrod.

We owe special thanks to Linda Fidnick and Carol Booth who generously offered their apartment to us (in a community where affordable housing is scarce), a gesture enabling five extended trips to Provincetown to collect interviews; to the Reverend Victoria Safford, minister of the Unitarian Society of Northampton and Florence, who volunteered to construct a special service interweaving stories from the manuscript and inspiring music from William Parker's "AIDS Songbook," performed in April, 1997; to Sadi Ranson, our editor at

Brookline Books/Lumen Editions, who quickly sensed the urgency and value of publishing this story.

Finally, we are profoundly indebted to our interviewees who entrusted us with their extraordinary stories. As we listened to their witness, one embedded in this dark plague, we were struck by how much light filled the room.

Introduction

In the first weeks of 1996 we rented a tiny crow's nest studio on the East End of Commercial Street. Three flights up outside wooden steps, our masthead vantage point was spectacular. The wide sun-lit bay lay at our feet, the dunes of Truro over our left shoulder, the town wharf and towering Pilgrim Monument over our right. Positioned to face the sea, anchored on a street also housing Stanley Kunitz, Norman Mailer, and Mary Oliver, we felt the essential resonances of Provincetown.

And then it began to snow. Thirty-six hours later, two feet of snow had accumulated, sixty-mile-per-hour winds buffeted our tiny studio, and the radio was calling this the "Blizzard of '96." Schools closed, airports stalled, most major cities on the East Coast were paralyzed.

From our little peep sight the bay churned and roiled, although the feared coastal flooding failed to materialize. The streets were muffled and still, the lights on the Pilgrim Monument barely visible, eerie in near whiteout conditions. It was easy to believe we were "on the edge of the world."

The weather was no more dramatic than the narratives we were to hear from the members of the community infected and affected by AIDS. During 1996 we interviewed those who live with HIV/AIDS, those who have lost partners, friends, family to the virus, those who grapple with "survivor guilt," those who offer support services, those who witnessed the dramatic arrival of protease inhibitors, the "magic cocktail" that suppresses, and some say, eradicates the virus. Our intention was not to homogenize these narratives into a single "representative" account, but rather to record a series of unique voices and life experiences that cross-hatch one another into a tapestry of community.

This is one story among many responses to a virus now in its sixteenth year in America and pandemic in its reach elsewhere. Provincetown's experience with AIDS is, understandably, dictated by its demographics. The overwhelming proportion of those infected with the virus are relatively young, white, well-educated gay men. A large percentage of that population has been gainfully employed in the past; most are aware of and able to make effective use of those entitlements available to them. They live in a rural "village" setting where virtually every member of a 3,300 person community has been directly and profoundly touched by AIDS. In Provincetown, it's not extraordinary to be gay, it's not extraordinary to be living with HIV, it's not extraordinary to be coping with repeated loss where grief is part of the landscape.

What *is* extraordinary is the communal response to the crisis. We discovered an intricate web of emotional, physical, and spiritual support implicit in all the stories we collected. "Touch one part of the web and the whole structure reverberates," one volunteer suggested; part of our task is to convey the delicacy and tensile strength of that web.

If the spirit of a place is shaped by its landscape, surely Provincetown's unique spirit is mirrored in its geographic extremes; "hard to get to and get out of," as Eugene O'Neill described his Provincetown home in 1919, the town is situated at the very edge of America where land's end reaches thirty-five miles into the Atlantic Ocean, where sunlight is so intense photographers adjust their cameras two f-stops, where storms and sand avalanches reconfigure all boundaries. Anyone who has driven Route 6 or 6A through the dunes of north Truro remembers that first wide-angle glimpse of the town: a sliver of land reaches out into the ocean like a crooked, beckoning finger, a shining town resting in its curvature.

The harbor must have attracted the Nauset Indians of the great Wampanoag Federation, European sailors and fishermen, shipwrecked survivors, and ultimately the Pilgrims who, diverted from their original destination in Virginia, touched land first in Provincetown in 1620. Moored in the harbor for 34 days in November and December of 1620, the Pilgrims decided against remaining in the area because it lacked fresh water and arable land, and headed west/southwest to Plymouth. They left not before they drafted the Mayflower Compact, a document describing the model community they intended to found, the one which ultimately expanded into the Massachusetts Bay Colony. Provincetown, just east of Plymouth and across the bay from Boston, was virtually ignored by mainland Massachusetts and remained a fringe society—a waystation for smugglers, renegade colonists, and roving Indians—well into the next century. The spirit that characterizes Provincetown's past and present can be caught in the dichotomy of its history: so remote as to attract and retain only the greatest risk takers, Provincetown was also the occasion for modeling "the city on the hill," the democratic haven for explorers who were fleeing from religious and social persecution. Risk and tolerance are forever wedded in Provincetown's history.

It's hard to be in present-day Provincetown and not feel that the place is alive with its literary predecessors. Thoreau was perhaps the first to popularize the place. A man who prided himself on "traveling widely in Concord," he journeyed to Cape Cod four times in the 1840s, once walking from Orleans to Provincetown to take meticulous note of the unusual geography. It was Thoreau who was inspired to write as he stood atop one of the sand ridges that separates Provincetown from the Atlantic Ocean, "A man may stand there and put all of America behind him."

During the early 1900s, Provincetown was a mecca for the artistic avant-garde and became known as Greenwich Village North. Active art schools and inexpensive summer lodgings close to the beach attracted young rebels and artists. Susan Glaspell, John Reed, Mabel

Dodge, were later joined by Edmund Wilson, John Dos Passos, e.e. cummings. Most significantly, in the summer of 1916 the then unrecognized young playwright Eugene O'Neill joined forces with the fledgling theater group, the Provincetown Players, and staged *Bound East for Cardiff* in a ramshackle wharf jutting out into the harbor. O'Neill stayed on in Provincetown for nine productive years; his meteoric rise to fame surely prompted other artists to seek in Provincetown the solitude, inspiration, and tolerance crucial to their creativity.

Charles Hawthorne inaugurated Provincetown's reputation as the nation's oldest continuous art colony. Starting in 1899, he taught painting to hundreds of students over a thirty-year period, emphasizing the beauty of the natural landscape and the extraordinary nature of "Cape light."

As it became less appealing to study art in Europe, especially after World War I seas grew too dangerous to cross, a number of American art colonies grew up, among them Woodstock, Taos, Carmel; by 1920, Provincetown was the most sizable of these colonies. In 1930 Hans Hofmann, arguably the most influential teacher in the history of American art, established his school in Provincetown. Artists who lived and worked in the Provincetown area for extended periods of time include Edward Hopper, Robert Motherwell, Mark Rothko, Marsden Hartley, Jackson Pollack, and Ben Shahn.

Provincetown's geographic isolation has always prompted its inhabitants to devise their own survival strategies. When fires posed real and frequent dangers Provincetown created, outfitted, and manned its own volunteer fire department. When a significant portion of HIV+ clients needed ongoing treatment at Boston hospitals, drivers and a van were recruited. When low-cost, high-nutritional meals became a priority, a program providing home delivery of hot meals emerged. When spiritual support groups and bereavement counseling became imperative, an AIDS ministry evolved at the local Universalist Meeting House. As several of our narrators suggested, Provincetown's isolation helps people lean closer to one another, helps them move "into the hard work of love."

There are many ways of articulating this story. There is the narrative of the progression of the disease itself, first visible in Provincetown in 1982 and claiming more than 385, one tenth of the permanent population, fourteen years later. There is the narrative of the coping strategies that people affected and infected have devised in the face of the epidemic. There is the narrative of loss and grief which draws its own trajectory and to which attention must be paid. There is the narrative of long term survivors some of whom have lost not one, but two circles of friends and loved ones. There is the dramatic arrival of the so-called "miracle drugs" offering a shining promissory note to some, tragically too late or too expensive for others. There is the mute testimony of those who have died and yet who are vividly alive, embedded in the lives of those left behind. And there is the ageless narrative of life and death, mirrored in the tide's fullness and withdrawal, forces which render Provincetown's rhythms archetypal. We chose to convey the felt truth of Provincetown's response to AIDS by recording first person accounts from those directly affected and infected, accounts drawn from all sectors of community life. Ours is not a scientific study where the database was subject to statistical analysis or qualifying criteria. Instead, we went to Provincetown five extended times over the course of 1996; we went as explorers, as listeners, and we were received with an astonishing degree of trust.

Why, we sometimes asked ourselves, were people able to open their hearts to strangers, to cut so quickly and unerringly to the marrow of this experience? Why did we so uniformly encounter cooperation rather than suspicion, assistance rather than reticence?

Perhaps in Provincetown, a community in deep mourning, it is simply inconceivable that anyone could be so fiendish as to exploit a tragedy of the magnitude of the AIDS epidemic. Perhaps, in some innocent way, we were simply lucky. Or perhaps Provincetown was ready, or eager, to give collective voice to its experience. Mark Doty, one of our narrators, observes that "the virus in its predatory destructions seems to underline the responsibility of living." That responsibility, in effect a mandate, propels this story.

Yoked to and illuminating that responsibility is the special angle of vision that loss generates. Although in one way or another each of our narrators claims partial vision—insight clouded by grief, vision impaired by fatigue, feeling insulated by necessary defenses—each sees *something* with the primary intensity accorded only to those who have experienced life as locked in a dance with death.

Would that we occupied a different moment in history—one that permits the luxury of hindsight, a look back at AIDS as an historic catastrophe which, in some cases, distilled the best in the human spirit. No one in 1996 has the luxury of hindsight, but each narrator who appears in these pages has a kind of searing sight. Light enough to live by.

Stories bear witness. At times they transcend the very language in which they are expressed. As Leslie Marmon Silko has reminded us, "Without the stories, we are nothing."

It is the stories we hold, turning them in our hands like trusted talismans.

Chapter One

The Provincetown AIDS Support Group

96–98 Bradford Street,
at the foot of the Pilgrim Monument

Situated at the corner of Bradford and Winslow Streets, the Province-town AIDS Support Group sits literally in the shadow of the towering Pilgrim Monument, a stone monument and observation tower built in 1907–08 to honor Provincetown's most famous early visitors, the Pil-grims, who after a perilous sixty-three-day voyage dropped anchor in Provincetown Harbor on November 21, 1620. Having achieved their landfall after a lengthy and frightening voyage, and having fled eco-nomic hardship and religious and social persecution, the Pilgrims as-sembled in the cabin of the Mayflower to draw up the Mayflower Compact, a document describing a system of governance based on self-determination and democratic participation.

Creating the kind of community that you wish to live in, provid-ing safe haven for those fleeing hardship and oppression, drafting as-surances of equal entitlements for all under the law, discovering power in self-determination: all lie at the roots of the Provincetown AIDS Support Group. In many ways the Provincetown AIDS Support Group is the hub of Provincetown's communal response to AIDS. Founded by a small group of concerned citizens in the vanguard of AIDS aware-ness in the early '80s—among them Mike Wright, Alan Wagg, Roger Baker, David Harris, William Scott—and co-chaired by Alice Foley and Preston Babbitt, PASG now, fourteen years later, serves 190 cli-ents (called consumers) on a budget in excess of $300,000 a year. It offers weekly support groups, transportation, meal preparation and delivery, weekly communal meals, counseling, social services and en-titlement advocacy, home care, the Boston van service, and most re-cently, coordination with Foley House and liaisons with Deaconess and Beth Israel Hospitals in Boston.

♨

PASG began largely as the result of shared perceptions of a "very scary and very secret" virus cropping up among a few gay men who had been forced undercover by their illness. Alice Foley, the town nurse, was among the first to encounter people with a "mysterious killing virus", several of whom were referred to Provincetown because "the gay com-munity will take care of its own." One day, while visiting a man who was ill and undercover, she met Preston Babbitt "going in as I was coming out. We made plans to meet and talk about our perceptions of what was going on." Babbitt, the owner of the Rose and Crown, a Victorian guest house on the West End, was a successful businessman and energetic community leader. He handled the business incorpora-tion while Foley began to gather and disseminate information about the disease. At first Foley and Babbitt, sensing the urgency of the problem, worked out of the trunks of cars, creating a mobile unit of sorts. As they realized that "a devastating disease was heading our way, one that was going to be affecting our friends and neighbors," they began wider-reaching efforts. "Provincetown was medically isolated, and a system of health and home-care services needed to be put in place," said Foley. She lobbied legislators to lift funding restrictions; she and Babbitt wrote grants which provided substantial operating monies, and gradually developed an organization which provides the current full range of services to those infected and affected by HIV/

AIDS. Preston Babbitt, the man with "the beautiful hair" (wavy hair he tied back and often braided with beads), the community activist, the Historic Commission member, the devotee of the Carnival Parade, each year marching in a more creative costume, the habitual attender of all the memorial services of those PASG had cared for, died of AIDS in 1990.

Alice Foley

Alice Foley is a force. Whether functioning as the Town Nurse, the Director of Public Health, a member of the Business Guild, a member of the town Finance Committee, she's someone who makes things happen. Possessed of a ready Irish wit and a ready Irish temper, her language is flavored by the Cambridge neighborhoods of youth. Her wildly funny anecdotes often feature colorful characters she's encountered at some of the places she's worked, like the Charles Street Jail.

An avid reader, her coffee table was stacked with books—novels, nonfiction, mysteries, science. She considers the Provincetown Library a "treasure house." Although retired as Town Nurse and executive Director of PASG, she is clearly in demand. Her answering machine, which she obligingly turned to "silent record" during our conversation, went off regularly with that succession of beeps and buzzes that signals incoming calls.

Alice Foley is the person you'd least like to encounter across the table at a Senate hearing as she presents a counter proposal to one you've just outlined. She is the person you'd most like to encounter if you had just been admitted to a hospital emergency room and she was the nurse in charge.

We asked her to describe the first cases of AIDS she saw in Provincetown as well as the early efforts to respond to this "mysterious virus."

> ❧ It was the early '80s, '82 maybe, that I was asked, as Town Nurse, to visit a sick young man living alone in town. When I went to see him, I discovered he had driven from Colorado to

Massachusetts General Hospital and then he had been referred out here. When I called the social worker who had referred him to ask why she would send a dying man to Provincetown she said, "because the gay community there will take care of him."

Later I saw my first Kaposi's [Kaposi's Sarcoma, or KS: skin lesions, often the first visible sign of AIDS in the early years]— a man, very, very sick, sitting in a rooming house, who looked like he had been splattered by a paint brush—big purple splotches of color all over his body. Later, as I thought back on it, I realized that there were other people who had AIDS as far back as the late '70s.

By 1986 AIDS was beginning to cost hospitals enormous amounts of money. The State Department of Public Health awarded grants to agencies who would provide in-home extended care for people with AIDS. We got one. That's when PASG could grow, even though it was the only small, locally based agency to receive such a grant. We got another one in 1989.

Pam: And in the meantime?

In the meantime it was a question of educating the community, of combatting fear, of learning as much about the disease as we could. This is, after all, a town that's accustomed to hardship. Maybe fifty percent of the population lives on unemployment in the winter and everybody learns to live on scanty resources. Before the tourist boom, good paying jobs were tremendously difficult—like the men who worked in the fishing boat holds, "lumpers" they're called, who stood all day in ice water to their knees. Hardship, resourcefulness are nothing new to Provincetown.

So we tried to take what was already in place and develop it. The EMTs, the Rescue Squad, for example had to overcome their fear of this virus so that dignified, gentle, courteous care could be offered to everybody. That wasn't easy. They're almost all straight men, family men, men who have to take time off work when emergency calls come in. And increasingly calls came from sick, gay men. Now the EMTs are absolutely wonderful; everybody says so.

As we came to realize the value of nutrition to people with AIDS we looked around and found a group of Portuguese women who prepared hot meals for the nursing home. At first I bought meals from them; later I wrote a grant to hire a cook and outfit the kitchen.

And always we were looking for ways to make sure Provincetown residents with AIDS could live as well as possible and die with dignity, be in a circle of friends, loved ones. We've had 385 or more people die from AIDS [between 1982 and 1996] in Provincetown, and only about a dozen have died in a hospital. That was really the purpose of the PASG.

Jeanne: What drew you to nursing?

I grew up in Cambridge [Massachusetts] in an Irish neighborhood very close to the Holy Ghost Hospital for the Incurably Ill. As kids we'd ride our bikes over there and sometimes make money taking one of the patients out for air on a gurney—a nickel a trip. Those words "For the Incurably Ill" were wrought in the iron archway. I used to imagine what it would be like, lying on your back, pushed through an archway that announced those dreadful words.

In the winter of 1995 Alice Foley and the PASG parted company in what can only be described as an acrimonious divorce. Not enough time has elapsed to confer perspective on the issues that precipitated the split, but it seems clear that Foley and some clients and staff at the PASG shared an increasingly embattled view of their mission.

Simply put, Alice Foley's training in nursing convinced her of the primacy of the medical model. She saw as her mandate the best possible care for clients *dying* of AIDS. As medical advances and protocols stretched the survival span of AIDS clients to eight, ten, in some instances twelve years, long-term survivors increasingly embraced self-empowerment models. They saw as their mandate the best possible care for clients *living* with AIDS. It was that difference in perspective that spawned numbers of conflicts: caring for a client versus self-determination, the rules and regulations of a medical model versus alternative therapies and self-directed decision making, executive power versus a client advisory board.

Following Alice Foley's departure, Len Stewart was elected Executive Director, a capacity he's served in for about one year. Len invited us to interview him and several other PASG staff members in early January of 1996. Len began his initial involvement in the PASG as a volunteer in 1987. He moved to Provincetown in 1981 after spending several years in Washington, DC working for freshman US Senator, Gary Hart, for Jerry Brown, and for the Carter administration. He decided to leave Washington and public policy work when Ronald Reagan was elected. "I wanted to get as far away from mainstream America, shopping malls, polyester clothes, and people who voted for Reagan as possible."

We arrive at the big double-decker building early in the day in mid-January, shortly after the Blizzard of '96 has dumped two feet of snow on Provincetown. The front entrance opens into a large common room outfitted with tables where several clients and staff members are quietly talking. One wall is lined with books, pamphlets, videos, and other educational materials about HIV/AIDS. A large-screen TV and several comfortable couches sit against another wall. A beautifully crafted walnut and glass display case which holds the Great Book, a leather-bound volume bearing the names of all Provincetown residents who have died of AIDS, attracts any visitor's eye. Two conference rooms are cordoned off from the common room, one a private space for group meetings, the other a client–case-manager office. To our right is the receptionist's desk and, situated at eye level, a small black and white board listing those who have most recently died of

AIDS. Two names with yesterday's and today's dates are posted.

Ginnine Principe, the chef and nutritionist, appears briefly to re-schedule her interview. It's about 11:30 A.M. and her hot lunch home delivery program is in full swing. Offices for various staff members, are housed upstairs. The common room hums with activity and with the buzz of simultaneous conversations, phone calls, and computer bells and whistles. The atmosphere is both welcoming and professional.

Len Stewart

Len Stewart led us through PASG's busy kitchen, up a front stairway, and through a succession of second floor offices. His office, a kind of communications center at the hub of the PASG staff offices—surrounded with ringing phones and spiraling computer screens—seemed an incongruous frame for his calm self-containment. His answers to questions were considered and complete, often rendered in complex, syntactically perfect sentences. Even his silences are complete units, unbroken by random *ohs* and *ahs*. In another life, you can imagine him as a speech writer for a liberal politician who needs to communicate his mission with accuracy and conviction. He has a quiet intensity, one that moves beneath the surface of the words.

      I began work as a volunteer at PASG probably in '87 or '88, and I came on staff I guess in 1992. I volunteered for jobs that nobody else wanted to do; I was volunteering to do things like organize an entire year's worth of empty beer bottles in order to collect the deposits. I specialized in tasks that did not re-quire much human contact. I'm a very shy, retiring guy, so that appealed to me. At the same time, my partner in 1989 became a client and so I got involved in the support group. We have something called the Family Care Program; it pro-vides some support services for the caregiver as well as for the person with AIDS, so I had all that additional contact.

Pam: What made you decide to come onto staff as a case manager, obviously very much a person-oriented job?

Gradually I realized that this was a town where things were happening that were matters of life and death to a lot of people. I was working for the town at that point, in the town manager's office, and I just decided I'd rather spend my life, personally and professionally, doing things I knew in the pit of my stomach and in my heart were of critical importance. I applied for a job at PASG and eventually I got one as a case manager. In that job you immediately develop an intense one-on-one relationship with a client, a partnership really. I like that approach to work, that one-on-one adds up to thirty or forty or fifty. It's a way of making a difference.

I also realized when my partner of that period died in 1989 how important it was to be surrounded by friends and loved ones at the end. He died in Florida where he had gone for warm weather in Fort Lauderdale, and I think he was desperate to get back here and be in a community of his loved ones. He had to take a bus across town to be treated at his health clinic. No one here would ever allow you to take a bus to a public health clinic to get treatment. We just take care of each other better than that.

Pam: What is it about Provincetown that created that web?

Well, for one thing it's the isolation. We've never been able to count on anybody else to fashion a solution to any of our problems, so we've just fashioned our own. I think it's part of the frontier mentality.

At the same time there's the gay and lesbian community which, as far as I know, has never gone anywhere else as refugees and ended up so quickly stitched into the fabric of the community. So that may explain the response to the AIDS crisis. The town was accustomed to taking care of its own and, additionally, the gay and lesbian community discovered somewhere on the planet where they were treated like first-class citizens. That's a powerful combination. When there's an epidemic threatening our brothers and sisters and neighbors, the web gets built.

Jeanne: So it's really a blended community.

Oh, yes, yes. And it's no artificial, politically correct tolerance for gay people in this community. After your first year here, you earn your way, you're welcomed as a valued citizen. Nobody trusts you before you've been through a winter here, however.

It's been just remarkable how everybody in the community has pitched in as the AIDS crisis evolved. They may contribute in terms of financial donations, in terms of plowing somebody's driveway, or by donating things to the auction, or cooking. Perhaps it's because every member of this community knows someone—knows someone *well*—who is living with AIDS. I wonder if that's true anywhere else?

At PASG we try to focus on living with AIDS. That may mean living the last few weeks of your life, or living the two years before the first opportunistic infection. Most of the staff here works to enable a person to live that particular day with AIDS—whether it's getting to Boston for a medical appointment, getting a nutritious hot meal, helping with food stamp problems—whatever. I have to admit that leaves a lot of us hurdling, hurdling, running down the road in this epidemic with little time to grieve, or figure out the impact on us. It's like being inside a football when somebody throws a pass.

If someone said, "Can you do this for ten years?", of course anybody would say, "No, I can't." But, looking back on it, we realize that we *have* done it for ten years, or for five years, or four years.

I'm a recovering alcoholic and I see meaningful work as a real need in my life, a necessity. I'm lucky because my job at PASG is to manage, and so I can, from moment to moment, focus on just dollars and cents, lose myself in a spreadsheet. As the director, I'm just the guy that tries to make sure that all these heroes that work here have desks, and light, and heat. The agency is full of really remarkable people and extraordinary programs. I don't need to be the center of the universe; I'm simply the guy who has to try to keep it all pasted together so that it continues to work.

Pam: Was it hard to move from being a case manager, directly involved with consumers, to "staring at a spreadsheet," as you put it?

It was very difficult. There is a moment, sometimes early on, sometimes later, that comes to every case manager where the two partners look each other in the eye. They establish a bond that tastes like, feels like—it *is* the truth. I miss that moment. And you know what? I miss organizing the beer bottles. I like to do the little pieces that contribute to the whole. The AIDS epidemic changed my perspective, it changed the scale of things. I don't care about a lot of things now—they're just secondary or tertiary to love, trust, empowerment, touching, supporting. And those are things I wouldn't have been able to talk to you about 15 years ago.

Jeanne: Where would you like to see the organization of PASG go? I suppose you'd like to see it go out of business.

I'd love to see it go out of business. But, if we have to continue to work in the face of this epidemic for a time, I would like to find a way to ease some of the constant negotiations. If, for example, we move from twenty-five lunches a day to thirty lunches a day, I have to do projections.

We are a rural group with an urban density of AIDS, and so every funding solution that people fashion when they hammer out state and federal compromises usually serves their purposes and doesn't serve ours. Negotiations, negotiations. I would like to see our needs addressed at the policy level. Then we can say without any qualifications or hedges, "here's what we have; it's for you." And people here can continue their extraordinary work.

ॐ

One of the people conducting that extraordinary work is Douglas Brooks, Director of Development at PASG, who lives out the challenges of being both "consumer" at PASG and simultaneously a paid staff member in charge of most fund-raising activities. Originally, Douglas came from Macon, Georgia, attended school in Atlanta, came to Provincetown for the summers of 1989 and 1990, and became a permanent resident in 1991.

Douglas Brooks

Douglas Brooks is at home inside his body in the way a dancer is. He moves with grace and balance; when he speaks, he opens his expressive hands and extends his arms as if choreographing the conversation. He has a warm, resonating laugh, one with genuine mirth in it, and he laughs most frequently at life's absurdities and daily ironies.

As our conversation had to be wedged into his lunch hour, at first Douglas struggled to balance answering questions with eating a delicious-smelling piece of quiche and portion of rice pilaf from Ginnine's kitchen. Finally he put the plate down, deciding to chew exclusively on questions.

Pam: How did you get involved with AIDS work?

Well, I ask myself if I would ever have gotten involved if it hadn't been forced on me. Before I left Atlanta I had a friend who was ill. His family wouldn't care for him. So I set up a buddy system—actually a circle of care for him. That was my first experience.

After I got here I worked at Gallerani's—the café. David Gallerani, who owned the place, had a program whereby a client from the Support Group came to have a meal with us everyday. He got a nutritious meal and we got to connect with the Support Group. I also helped David do a communal meal here once. So, when some of my friends decided they wanted to entertain by doing a drag show, I suggested that we do it for the Support Group. It was a great success; we raised a couple thousand dollars, I think, and we ended up representing the Support Group at other fund-raising functions. By December I was working here as a paid full time staff member in the capacities of program coordinator and case manager. When I retired from that I stayed on as the fund raiser.

Pam: How difficult is it to be both a consumer—attending groups, taking advantage of some of the services—and also being a staff member?

For a long time I was the only person in that dual role. I am HIV+ and this is the only agency in town that offers services; I also work at that agency. Trying to maintain boundaries in Provincetown is difficult at best, and sometimes I was very torn between my two roles—especially if I saw something at the Support Group that I didn't think was in the consumer's best interest. And, at first, I was still actively drinking. I hadn't dealt with my own diagnosis.

Pam: When were you diagnosed?

In 1990, and for a while all I did was self-medicate. When I did begin to see a therapist I think it was only eight or nine weeks before the therapist said, "Will you go to AA?"

Jeanne: Was giving up drinking, especially at that time, difficult?

I'm still waiting for it to be difficult. People say it should be and here I am two years later still waiting. I think I was just so ready to be emotionally healthy. I was ready to have the misery removed. I already had the foundation of believing in a higher power, in God, of relying on a faith. So that wasn't something I had to learn. I had all the tools, I had just put them aside for a while.

As soon as I moved into recovery I could feel hope and energy returning. I could see other things I wanted to pursue. I took a leave from last September to May to go back to school; I'm finishing a degree in Human Services and Counseling Psychology at Lesley College.

I don't see HIV as a gift, but I do think it changes your perspective. Life is a precious gift, it is fleeting, and you can't waste time. [He coughs.] You've probably noticed I have some congestion today. Well, people who are not positive wake up in the morning and may notice they have some chest congestion. If I wake up with congestion I have to take deep breaths to determine what kind of a cold it is; I need to know if there's a possibility of bronchitis or pneumonia. Day to day I have to get kick-started in the morning. That makes for priorities.

Jeanne: Do you have support from your own family?

Yes, oh yes. I grew up in a family where support, being of service, was the rule. Both of my parents were very involved in church, community work. My father died in 1989, but my mother knows my HIV status and she is incredibly supportive. She's seventy-two years old and when I talk with her she inquires about my health, then moves very quickly to something encouraging, empowering. The first thing she said when I told her what my status was, "Don't let this beat you. I came back from cancer. We come from fighting stock, so hop to it."

Pam: What changes have you seen in the town, the attitudes of people in the five years you've been here?

People have lost not one but two circles of friends. They lost the first circle in the '80s and then a whole other circle in the early '90s. It amazes me how these people can still come in here, deliver lunches, drive the van to Boston, continue their level of giving. PASG has grown to the point where we serve 190 people—that is 190 people who have gone through an intake and have a positive HIV status. Then there's the whole widening group of the affected—I'd estimate that we reach half of the permanent population in Provincetown. I'll be conservative and say we reach, in one way or another 1,500.

Sometimes it seems really screwy, what you have to learn to do in this epidemic. I'm thirty-three years old and I know how to say good-bye to dying friends. I'm good at it. That's twisted learning.

But the support is real. At the Meeting House, where most of the memorial services take place, we always say, "If you're not in the front pew being the chief mourner, the immediate family, then you're in the second pew putting your arms around the people in the front pew." We've had to learn to give grief its respect or it will knock the shit out of us.

And we're also fortunate to have wonderful professionals in the fight, choosing the fight. With all their credentials and experience they could go to Boston and make $175 an hour. Instead, they stay out here and make "chump change."

A lot of them are women. So strong. The women. The women. They just decided they had to take care of their brothers. Lifting them, and turning them, and listening to them, and holding hands.

Pam: Can I ask you this question; is it isolating to be an African American man in Provincetown, essentially a white community?

Oh, you noticed. [Laughter] HIV+, African American, gay ... not many options? Well, actually I hadn't realized it very much until the last year. I was in Los Angeles for a conference and had dinner with seven other African American gay men engaged in doing this work. It was a wonderful experience. A treat. And I thought on the plane coming home, "Being with your own people isn't supposed to be an exception." But, Provincetown is like no other place. I call Cape Cod Bay my front yard and the Atlantic Ocean my backyard.

One of the things that makes me sad about dying with HIV is that I really wish I could be here fifty years from now to see what happens. To see how we did. To study the history, pull the statistics together. We can't see it now. We're in it, we're in it.

✌

Jackie Freitas, a volunteer at PASG since 1986, one of those "strong women" Douglas mentioned, currently drives the van to Boston for clients who have scheduled medical treatments at Boston hospitals and clinics.

Jackie came to Provincetown in 1986 and has worked in various capacities with PASG, particularly as the driver and coordinator for the Boston transportation program, one that now makes stops for AIDS clients who have chosen medical treatment in the Boston area. She had just returned from Nantucket where she received an award for meritorious service from the Tri-County AIDS Consortium the day we spoke.

Jackie Freitas

Equipped with the kind of Boston accent even a resident of South Dakota could identify, Jackie Freitas describes her extraordinary service with matter-of-fact, short, descriptive sentences. "I was here; I saw the need; I did the job," she says in one way or another, implying that any ordinary citizen under siege of the epidemic would do the same. A kind of invisible energy appears to carry her: nothing about driving the van is impossible to manage, nothing about respite care is too exhausting. It is only when she speaks of the animals that sick clients have had to abandon to long days of inactivity and waiting, that you sense her frustration with this seemingly interminable disease. She has a special connection with animals and their mute grieving; their long hours of waiting seem to mirror her own elongated, steady sorrow. She came to the interview carrying a fresh supply of IAMS dog biscuits, an accompaniment to all of her walks around town.

✧   I was first sensitized to this kind of work while my mother was dying of cancer in 1984. She had the most wonderful hospice nurse whom I admired greatly. It was watching that nurse work, sitting with my mother, listening to her talk that I came to understand how to support someone who is also asking you to let them go. My mother actually said to me, "I need somebody with me who will let me go." She also suggested that I come to Provincetown. I was working as a tech writer for Raytheon but had vacationed in Provincetown for years. My mother said "You love Provincetown. Provincetown loves you. Why don't you just relocate there when I'm gone?" It's true; I love Provincetown. I call the ocean the "mother's blood" and I feel completely at peace when I'm surrounded by it.

In 1986 the disease was just in our face. Pneumocystis pneumonia was taking people quickly, so quickly. I started to help—first as Alice Foley's secretary. Alice knew almost immediately that this was a devastating virus, some new terrible strain we hadn't encountered before. For example, she said that KS rarely affects young men, and here it was in all these young, gay men.

There was great fear at first, as you can imagine, trying to treat something you hadn't seen before. So you had to work around that. At first even the medical people were terrified; they wore masks, gloves, hats—they looked like astronauts. But many people too were guided by what was in their hearts. Preston Babbitt was one of those. He had ... a great spirit, and he was a good business man. For a time he and Alice worked out of trunks of cars; PASG was a mobile unit. Here were suffering people, some of them completely abandoned, very sick, in need of companionship. After we knew how it was transmitted, the fear eased.

But the needs grew. And I decided to just apply myself, do what was needed, pass no judgments. I guess I'm a person who does what's required. So if I know somebody needs twenty-four-hour care, I'll do a couple of shifts a week. Or I'll be responsible for their animals. Their dogs and cats don't need to feel unloved just because their people are sick. Pets are of great concern to the sick; often they represent their families, their best friends. So I care for the animals, walk them, feed them, love them. I always carry treats in my pockets.

And I became the transportation person. I love to drive, I know Boston well, so I began to drive the van. Driving the van you hear everything. Everything. There's the fear and the anger that goes with being very sick. The frustration. I just listen. Clients choose their own treatments too, so I hear about that. I pick up clients all along Route 6—in Orleans, Hyannis, all the way to the [Sagamore] bridge now, so I'm seeing lots of new people too. Sometimes I get close to people. There was, for example, a woman I drove for quite a long time that I got close to, became her power-of-attorney, etc. A transsexual. She was beautiful. Gorgeous. But in her AIDS treatment they took away her hormones and she went back to being a man. I think she died more of a broken heart than of AIDS. You know, everybody has a personal truth, and we have to learn how to honor that.

Pam: Can you see yourself continuing in this work indefinitely?

Of course we all wish this epidemic would end. It's maddening when you see new populations dealing with the virus, when you realize it just goes on and on and on. I'll do this work as long as I'm needed. I've asked myself what other kinds of AIDS work I could do—and I realize I couldn't work with children with AIDS. That's just heart-wrenching to me. But I think I could work with adult women—needle users, prostitutes, that population. And if we ever see the end of this epidemic, I'd like to work with an organization like HOW [Helping Our Women], working with chronic and life threatening illnesses that affect women. I could be of use there.

☙

Ginnine Principe

Focus. Centeredness. The still point in a turning world: these are the kinds of energy that flow from Ginnine Principe. Perhaps as the result of the mind-body-spirit explorations she's studying, or perhaps as the result of her training as a professional chef, it's possible to imagine Ginnine—with very little notice—preaching to the five thousand or feeding the five thousand. The spirit and the body are intimately connected by multiple networks, in her view, and feeding one necessarily replenishes the other.

She listened carefully to our questions, often complimenting us on their difficulty or appropriateness. Her own responses were thoughtful and invariably open-ended, as if her search for answers was just beginning. The pain, the racked beauty evident in both places where she serves—as a lay minister in the Unitarian Universalist Church, as the Food and Nutrition Coordinator for PASG—seem, by some strange alchemy, to produce an alloy of strength, which is surprisingly sustaining, and very precious to her.

☙   I was born and raised in Long Island, New York, in a little fishing village very much like Provincetown. I went away to school, studied a variety of things, but couldn't decide on what I really wanted to do. So I left college to pursue culinary arts and became a chef. I worked for the restaurant business in Manhattan for seven years, burnt out, became a consultant. I made a tremendous amount of money and decided that I'd either move to San Francisco or Provincetown and live in a gay and lesbian community where I could feel comfortable, safe. Once I got here I realized that I was actually undergoing a huge spiritual awakening. That was '92, so I'm in my fourth year here.

My life has changed drastically since I've been here. Drastically. I met a dear friend, Ross Thompson, who was also on a spiritual path centered around healing. Together we explored all types of alternative therapies including food and nutrition, herbs, massage, body work, yoga, different religious leaders.

I'm asthmatic and have been since birth. It's almost killed me several times. So I felt a very strong bond with people living with AIDS; we share a lot of similar issues.

I got very involved with the Unitarian Universalist Meeting House two years ago—work that includes being on the worship committee, being involved in fund raising, now being part of the ministry. I was able to open up once I made that commitment to be in service, to help people. I had no desire to be in the restaurant business. But what do I do with all this training with food? How do I fuse that with the healing sensibilities? All of a sudden this job appeared at PASG looking for a food and nutrition coordinator. Boom, there I went.

Pam: So you had never done work with people with HIV/AIDS in the past?

Only as a volunteer, back in New York. When I was nineteen years old I was working as a student intern with a gay/lesbian publication on Long Island called *Parlez.* They brought me in to help start up the publication of a newspaper called *Equal Times,* something which didn't really go anywhere. But that was an important year for me; the man who mentored me was Rich Amato, a figure very involved in the local political scene in 1984–85. He was one of the earliest AIDS activists in New York, and he was also the first person I knew who turned up HIV+. He got sick and died very quickly, a few years later. So it was that experience, it was the activism wing from which I came into this pandemic.

Pam: Your volunteer work here was mostly via the UU church, however, not PASG?

That's right. I would work the auction at PASG once a year; I threw myself into helping HOW; they were the newer organization, the one that was in worse shape financially at the time. But most of my volunteer time went to the church. I saw that as the house through which most were going to pass eventually.

Jeanne: What exactly is "lay ministry"? How did it come about?

Our new minister, Reverend Jennifer Justice, went to work right away putting a lay ministry into place. It's composed of folks who can offer pastoral care, companion work, work with the elderly, represent the congregation as a delegate, become a chaplain—a kind of student minister. I think a lot of us who are drawn to this work are really drawn to the ministry. Quite frankly, if I could go next month to theological school I probably would, but I'm also immersed, committed to the work I'm doing at PASG.

As a chaplain as the Meeting House I do union ceremonies which is both a tremendous honor and a balance to the work I do at the support group.

Pam: Tell us about your work at PASG.

I run the food and nutrition program which is composed of a lunch delivery program called Afternoon Dish. My volunteers deliver a hot meal of at least three, sometimes five courses, to home-bound clients five days a week. We run at about twenty clients, and in many cases we stock people up to get through the weekend. We go between Provincetown and Orleans at present. Two drivers come in every day; one stays in town and the other shoots out of town to hit clients in Truro, Eastham, Wellfleet, and Orleans. It's a very important program for all of the home-bound, and obviously it allows us to get a volunteer into the house to eyeball the situation every single day.

Then we have a communal meal every Tuesday night called Local Flavor where we invite in a guest chef from the community to prepare a meal. It can be anybody who is willing—from the grandmas at the Catholic Church to a chef from a Provincetown restaurant. That meal is open to any consumer; they can bring a partner, a family member, a friend.

Pam: Do you sit down with each new client and talk about nutrition needs?

We do a nutritional intake and talk about dietary restrictions, issues around food, the importance of good nutrition, their specific concerns. Sometimes talking about food seems to uncover other needs: their battles with depression, with loneliness. So when they say, "I don't have any appetite," or "Nothing seems appealing," what they're really saying is, "I don't want to live anymore." And there are a lot of trust issues that come up around food. Occasionally clients will call, some repeatedly and say, "Hey, what's in this? Are you sure there's no X, Y or Z?" That's fear talking, so they need to double check with me, trust me.

I have specific diets, restricted diets, to work around—and, of course, those problems specific to AIDS; repeated opportunistic infections, thrush, chronic diarrhea, loss of appetite. And when a client begins to experience renal failure it becomes a real challenge, since that means eliminating sodium, potassium and protein.

I work in a kitchen that's a huge traffic zone. You saw it, lots of traffic all the time. People have come to understand how I feel about food. At first when people would come through my kitchen arguing about something I'd tell them that they need to take that elsewhere. We can't have that kind of energy going into the food.

They began looking at each other like "Oh-oh. What kind of New Age plane did she jump off of and why is she here?" But over time they've begun to understand me. Feeding people is a very, very spiritual thing for me. These meals and the volunteers that bring them are sometimes the highlight of a client's day, the only person he'll see that day.

We've done some special holiday meals, like the Passover Seder. PASG and all the local churches co-sponsored a Seder of Hope—a "Seder for people touched by AIDS," which was written by Gary Reinhardt and the Am HaYam congregation. That was a moving experience. It was held on April 10th, the last night of Passover, at the United Methodist Church. I helped coordinate the food and it was open to the whole community. The Seder was a retelling of the ancient Haggadah, the story of captivity and liberation, to include, actually to parallel the story of the AIDS epidemic, its bondage and hope.

There is an incredible amount of grief around this work. The loss is tremendous, but—let's see if I can put this into words—the greater the loss, the greater the pain, the more open I feel myself become. I know that some people experience the opposite; they lose their ability to feel. But, for me, one by-product of all this pain is the possibility for real joy.

I don't see myself as continuing indefinitely. It would be nice if I was out of a job soon. But I feel I also would like to work with a more diverse population, with women and children also. I don't know if you know this, but the statistics say that by the end of the year there will be 20,000 children in New York who will be orphaned by AIDS. I don't know that I've actually digested that information yet, but I think about those kids and what their futures are going to be like. And the women with AIDS are starting to come out of the closet a little bit more. You've got to understand that the dynamic is a lot different for them; lots of them are coming from the IV drug user population and they're not treated well. They're being asked to become visible in primarily a gay community that they may have little experience with. That can be quite a challenge. There are two women clients now and have been about seven women clients all together. One of them is on the front page of the *Cape Cod Times* today. The other is a resident of Foley House.

Pam: Can you tell us a little about Foley House? How does it work?

Foley House is an assisted living program modeled after assisted living programs in other parts of the state. There are ten bedroom units, two kitchens; each resident has his or her own refrigerator, little microwave. There's a twenty-four-hour staff available to ensure nursing and counseling support. There's also a resident support staff. These are folks who have been trained in what is actually required to assist people with AIDS in their living environment. It's not separate from PASG, but a part of a larger housing program. I have many of these residents on my meal program. But we're also encouraging residents of Foley House to prepare their own meals. I did a series called "Cooking for One" which got some interested. And residents who fit the criteria can come in from other parts of the state. This is not confined to Provincetown, or the Cape. Some of the old boundaries are being erased.

There are some signs of new hope on the horizon; new self-empowerments, new medications, Foley House, the Seder of Hope. Hope. Now that's a beautiful thing.

Although it is only mid-afternoon when we leave the Support Group building, the lights on the Pilgrim Monument shine brightly. Remnants of the holiday season, they wink through the gathering darkness. In the winter, dusk comes swiftly to Provincetown, and the air grows heavy with the threat of snow.

We walk down the short hill to the base of the Monument to see the bas-relief depicting the signing of the Mayflower Compact. Bradford's *History*, told in retrospect, is an account filled with the plagues and hardships that were to decimate the early settlers: disease, malnutrition, exposure. He fails, however, to detail the drowning of his own wife, Dorothea, in Provincetown Harbor, an incident that has prompted much speculation about her possible suicide, a casualty of acute isolation. Hardships not withstanding, there he stands caught in the act of signing the Compact, an act symbolizing the Pilgrim's unflagging conviction that their larger mission was to create a shining "City on the Hill," a community free from persecution and intolerance.

We walk the long mile back to the East End, paralleling the bay. The water is calm tonight, accented only by the soulful, half-strangled cries of gulls. We can see all the way home.

Chapter Two

Universalist Meeting House

236 Commercial Street

Spring has not yet opened its warm, wet canopy. Temperatures in mid-May hover in the low 50s as about two hundred marchers gather at the St. Mary of the Harbor Episcopal Church on the East End for the Thirteenth Annual AIDS Memorial and Mobilization. A strong ocean breeze wafts the hair of the marchers as they lean close, lighting green candles from one another, protecting the flames with plastic cups. Seemingly without perceptible signal, the procession snakes onto Commercial Street and begins the mile walk to the Universalist Meeting House. The line moves slowly, three or four abreast, sometimes joined by late comers who fold themselves inconspicuously into the group. Small children march with their parents; several well-behaved dogs trot beside their owners; some couples walk hand in hand; one woman walks fiercely forward, her companion pulling a portable oxygen tank beside her.

Conversation is minimal, low-pitched. One woman starts to sing the first verse of "We Are a Gentle, Angry People" in a pure contralto, but not many others know the words and her voice dies away.

As the procession nears the town center others begin to appear at curbside: waiters, shopkeepers, cooks, young couples holding children on their shoulders, all standing in silent witness. Second-story residences come alive as people lean out of windows or sit in darkened rooms, their faces illumined by a burning candle.

The doors of the Universalist Meeting House, white clapboard and immense, stand open. The sound of slow, steady drumming—more a heartbeat than a dirge—cuts the air in insistent measures. Marchers turn into single file to enter the church, pulling candles in close under their faces so that they look lit from within.

The sanctuary is dark and filled to capacity. Several speakers, among them Ed Frock, the Assistant Minister for AIDS Ministry at the Meeting House and Douglas Brooks, the Director of Development at PASG, reflect on strategies for converting anger and grief into productive action. If their messages constitute the "Mobilization" part of the service, the "calling of the names" serves as the "Memorial" counterpart. Four readers alternate in calling out names from the Great Book, a large, leather-bound volume permanently housed at the Provincetown AIDS Support Group, which contains the names of all Provincetown residents who have died of AIDS since 1983. The Great Book records twenty-six pages of names. As the names are called candles are lighted on either side of the pulpit. It is as if absence and presence are intertwined.

Members of the congregation are invited to invoke the names of others who have died of AIDS that they wish to remember. At first, voices call out names haltingly, intermittently. But, steadily, in the flickering sanctuary, the names begin to rise in mounting crescendo, one tumbling upon another, and another, and yet another, in a verbal fugue of grief and memory.

Provincetown resident and composer John Thomas's "Beloved Companions," a cantata for choir and orchestra, closes the service. Seated high in a rear balcony the choir flings these ringing words, adapted from Richard Lattimore's translation of *The Iliad*, out over the sanctuary:

> *Rise up with us, now go forward*

Nobody else stands behind us
remember your fury, valor
remember your dying brothers

As the music draws to a close a lone bell tolls in the tower, the long deliberate requiem strokes reverberating out over wide water—rolling, rolling.

The Universalist Meeting House congregation, first gathered in 1829, was substantial enough by 1851 to build its own church. The Greek Revival structure was built by local ship carpenters, constructed mainly of wood from Provincetown.

Its light tower, made of Sandwich glass, burns nightly in tribute to fishermen lost at sea. The pews, fabricated from Cape Cod pine and imported mahogany, are decorated with numbered medallions made from carved sperm whale teeth. The steeple leans perceptibly to the right, a fact most tourists notice as they compose photographs, and a fact most Unitarian Universalists ponder with a mixture of amusement and dismay.

By far the most extraordinary feature of the church is the *trompe l'oeil* painting of the sanctuary, a mixture of shading and highlighting which transforms the boxy room into a faux marble interior with a dramatic apse framing the pulpit.

Placed almost exactly at the town's center, the Universalist Meeting House attracts the eye because of its imposing architecture, its stretch of well-tended green grass (an actual "yard," a rarity on Commercial Street), the nightly lighted beacon shining from the tower, and the message it communicates to all visitors: "People gather here in a spirit of acceptance and caring—to search freely together for spiritual wholeness and responsible living. In a world of too much hate, intolerance, and indifference, the Universalist Meeting House stands as an island of safety, nurturing and love."

The Reverend Jennifer Justice has completed two years of ministry here and the Reverend Ed Frock one year as Assistant Minister for AIDS Ministry. Both are graduates of Harvard Divinity School, drawn to the ministry after pursuing other careers for a time; both accepted the call to the Universalist Meeting House shortly after their ordinations. Both support a grueling schedule of pastoral counseling and care, sermons and church duties, support groups, liaison work with other clergy, officials, health care workers in town, and a series of memorial services which occur with staggering frequency.

Jennifer Justice

Jennifer Justice has a disarming way of turning a question back to the questioner, in effect, interviewing the interviewer. Trained as professional storyteller, she uses her storyteller skills advantageously in an interview; her answers are full of dramatic pauses and effective pacing. Traces of the North Carolina of her birth remain in her speech and also in her way of greeting and bidding farewell to friends and parishioners. She favors the Southern Hello-and-Farewell method—an elongated duet in which both parties say hello and good-bye at least three times before actually getting on with it. The graciousness of this practice slows her crowded schedule, so she's always running a little behind; folks adore her for it. "Reverend JJ," as her parishioners call her, charms an audience, both in the sense of delighting and pleasing them, and also in the shaman's sense of making them recognize their magic.

Her story commences as she locates the nexus between storytelling and her decision to become a UU minister.

    Actually there were three paths that led me from storytelling to the ministry. The first stories that I told were stories of Holocaust survivors which I told in synagogues in order to honor and preserve memories. Part of the function of storytelling is to create community and that was the second path. I love that part of storytelling since it helps us know what's universal in us all. But unfortunately in professional storytelling that sense of community was transitory; I came in, told the story, went on to another place. I found I wanted to stay in a community the way storytellers used to do—from birth, to life, to death. The third path emerges from my own spiritual tradition which is an amalgam of Sufism, Tibetan Buddhism, and Hindu Shivaism. In that tradition everybody is God. So in storytelling I could speak to God in everybody. I wanted that to be my job, to think more deeply about theology and its traditions, and to be in a community which invited that exploration, wanted me to do that.

My mom was a Unitarian the last twenty years of her life. I needed a tradition that would allow me to draw primarily from Hinduism, from my storytelling background, and allow me to be a lesbian. There is none other! I'm really grateful that Unitarian Universalism exists. And my grandfather and great-grandfather were southern Baptist ministers—so that tradition was in place.

I went to Harvard Divinity School which is where I met Ed Frock, and interviewed for this position the day I was ordained.

I knew Provincetown since my partner and I have had a house in Wellfleet for seven years and I did my student ministry in Brewster. While I was in divinity school two friends from this community died of cancer. I performed their memorials, so the congregation knew me through those services and invited me to candidate here.

Pam: Did you have a sense of the scope of the epidemic before you came?

In a way I did, and I'd done my own grieving over the course of some years. Anyone who's been coming to Provincetown over the years has noticed how the gay men were disappearing. I remember being struck by their absence. But actually the congregation didn't voice it as a need or concern during my interview.

Pam: Don't you find that astonishing?

> When your needs aren't met for a long time you forget both that you have them and you forget how to invent strategies for meeting them. They didn't have a grief support group when I came to town. There was a therapy group for clients at PASG.

Jeanne: And everybody was just taking care of it individually?

> Or not, or *not*. After—actually *during* my third sermon, I realized that I faced an entire community in drastic crisis. My first two sermons I planned as high-impact because I was candidating them; I wanted them to hire me. They cried, they laughed, they showed lots of emotions. My third sermon was an old sermon. I didn't want them to have high expectations all the time, so I was going to do a less hot-shot sermon, something quite regular. The congregation went through exactly the same emotional process, crying within the first few minutes. I realized then what an emotional process they were going through. No matter what sermon I gave, they were expressing what they would during a memorial service. So I started to plan my sermons as if they were a part of an ongoing memorial service, in a way, in order to allow that emotional process to unfold.
>
> I started a support group and insisted on talking about AIDS … talking about it from the pulpit, because the silence was horrible. It was unbearable. If you think about groups who are going to empathize with the AIDS epidemic you think of Holocaust survivors or abuse survivors.

Pam: Trauma?

> Trauma and silence. Trauma and silence …

Jeanne: What led you to identify a need for an AIDS ministry?

> This congregation has a history of ministers who have come and gone, moved on very quickly, moved rapidly into burnout. I knew when I came here that they couldn't, as a congrega-

tion, stand to lose another. When I realized what this congregation was going through, the needs of this church, the work that was required to meet those needs, I realized I was going to burn out too. They had to have another full-time minister. And they had to have those needs addressed.

In my congregation you look out on any given Sunday and you're facing at least fifty percent HIV+ or people living with AIDS; you're looking at 100 percent affected by AIDS. You can't claim to be a church and refuse to address those needs.

I think the impossibility of doing the work alone came home to me when I met Paul, shortly after coming here. He died of AIDS when he was twenty-nine. I can still cry over Paul anytime. His ashes sat in my office for a year before they were scattered. I'd come in everyday and say "Hi, Paul."

He's the first person who said to me, "The only reason I can figure out for going through this is that our purpose in life is to grow closer to unconditional love." That's what his dying process taught him. And I couldn't find enough spaces in the schedule to see him. I was doing two memorial services a month, plus all the other duties. I would see him every two weeks or so. So rarely. And every time I would go he would say, "Oh, I'm so glad you're here. I know how busy you are." It was unbearable. His was a totally generous heart.

Pam: When you first came, recognized the needs, recognized the silence—did you meet any resistance? Was there anyone who said "you're going too fast, we don't need this yet"?

The congregation gave me permission from the beginning. Actually, the only place I met resistance was the Unitarian Universalist Association [UUA]. They thought I was going too fast, that I was biting off more than I could chew. I met with the president of the UUA after I'd been here two months and I told him that we were failing this congregation, that we had been failing it for years. And they gave me a major grant! Most of the grass roots of the UUA has been terribly responsive. And this district has been hugely responsive. Three or four congregations in this district have already had fund raisers for the AIDS ministry. And there are other denominations in the immediate community who work closely with us—George Welles at St. Mary's, and Gary Reinhardt and the Jewish congregation Am HaYam.

Jeanne: Is there any formal coalition of churches in the community?

Yes, there is a formal coalition and very good relations among the churches, I would say. But it's still difficult for us to do things together. We tried, for example, to do several things jointly the first year I was here. We always do an Easter Sunrise Service together. Our congregation is very diverse; even for a UU congregation it's unusual. We have Trinitarian Christians here, Agnostics, twelve-steppers, Naturists, Unitarian Christians ... I mean, we're taking Universalism to where it really asks you to go. But we discovered we can only do one directly "Christian" service a year. For Christians that's insufficient, but for Jews and Agnostics it's probably too much. Instead of trying to do joint services, we thought it better to allow different congregations to sponsor events, so that they can do them authentically, in their own traditions and worship styles. I would say that we meet together less, but now I believe we are a more authentic coalition.

After I was here only five months—and out of some powerful felt need—a group of church leaders, AIDS service organization directors, and therapists started to meet monthly to address some of the common needs. Some of the earlier fractures between PASG and PWA began to heal; some of the factions decided to pull together

Pam: Do you see homophobia and fear in action in this community?

They are in action in every community. But in this community you have to understand a very difficult economic situation exists. People are in severe economic stress. The fishing industry is essentially gone; many long-time residents can't afford to live here any longer. Gay men and women, outsiders mostly, are buying up valuable business and residential property. Anytime you have economic stress you have anger: anger that has to attach itself to something—a scapegoat. When long-time residents see themselves displaced by absentee landlords, or seasonal residents, most of them gay, those people became easy targets.

George Welles

George Welles, vicar of St. Mary of the Harbor Episcopal Church, came to Provincetown in January of 1989. He came from Hartford to the Cape in 1982, serving first in the large Episcopal church in Barnstable. During that time he was very active with Hospice of Cape Cod, preparation he considers a bridge to his work with the AIDS community. Welles arrived at the height of political activism in Provincetown, when divisiveness among groups was growing, when anger, what he calls "the rage of the illness" was spilling into the streets.

ACT-UP, the radical activist organization that attempts to force the federal government to respond to the AIDS crisis, came to Provincetown in 1989. Outraged by lack of access to health care, by the government's indifference to new research and alternative therapies, and by the ever-rising death toll, ACT-UP used marches, sit-ins, and "die-ins" to attract public attention to their cause. Their widely publicized march on Commercial Street in the summer of 1989 wounded many Provincetown residents who had always thought of their community as among the most responsive to AIDS in the nation.

Welles's story fleshes out Jennifer Justice's observations about "scapegoating" and the efforts by community leaders, clergy, and health care providers to turn rage into productive social action. The completion of Foley House, a ten-unit assisted living facility for clients living with AIDS, is one example of productive social action. Foley House, in some ways, rose like the phoenix from the ashes, as the construction crew who were engaged to renovate an existing structure, in fact demolished the entire building.

The power of his handshake and the way he balances on the balls of his feet suggest the sports coach that he's been in the past. There's something of the same agility and athleticism in the way he fields questions—upending them, flipping them, stretching them—inspecting what is inside and worth addressing. He seems equally at home inside the wood-dark interior of St. Mary of the Harbor Church, or outside on the sunny expanse of beach that fronts the church and vicarage. His "faith journey," as he calls his life experience, has taken him to varied places—a stint working as a teacher and coach at the Westminster School; a long residence in Hartford, Connecticut, where he and his wife raised their two biological daughters and adopted several African American children while living in a predominantly black neighborhood; a period of time when he worked not only as vicar in Barnstable, but also for Hospice of Cape Cod. His life reflects what Thomas Merton called the "unity of faith and action."

When I came here from Barnstable I knew obviously that there was a large gay population, that there would be a high incidence of HIV/AIDS. I knew that coming out of the Hospice experience I'd make immediate contact with the AIDS Support Group, that that would be a natural fit. There was no hesitation in translating what I understood to be my faith journey into concrete action. I not only got involved there, but I also got appointed to the Finance Committee, eventually was elected to the School Board, got on the Housing Authority as well. So immediately we moved into the life of the town. I don't think I understood that it was as fear filled as it was at that time.

The year before I came was when the break occurred within the life of the AIDS Support Group that produced the Provincetown Positive Coalition. This was the first break and the fault line seemed to be drawn between the dominant personalities of Alice Foley and John Perry Ryan. Perhaps that sounds more definite than it should; they were the key person-alities associated with each position and the war escalated, became wild and vicious. ACT-UP came in that following summer [1989], into fertile ground for even more contentious-ness; it produced an explosion from which I thought we'd never recover. It was terrible, and yet I think it was an incred-ibly cathartic moment that enabled us to take a quantum leap ahead. It really facilitated an eruption that was ultimately cleansing.

But that summer, people's behavior with one another was indescribably cruel. And exploitation was everywhere. Imag-ine asking clients from the support group, PWAs, who should be lifting everybody's behavior to a different level, to carry a parade banner indicting the town: "Silence is Death" it read.

Yet I find myself being able to identify with their rage, with the frustration and the impotence, with the anger at being part of a system that was taking all too long to come up with new medicines or protocols to treat the disease.

And then there were others who thought that AIDS vic-tims were getting what they deserved; their lifestyle was so corrupt. So there was that rhetoric of hate swirling around.

I found myself in the middle of the parade irrationality. St. Mary's name was on the parade permit. Keith Boyles, a sum-mer minister hired by the interfaith coalition in town, got drawn into the parade's planning stages through his street min-istry. He didn't realize there was a lot of behind the scenes planning going on, that the ACT-UP guys who were here had their own agenda. He got caught in divided loyalties—and evidently he felt he couldn't even come confidentially to some of us who were on the board of the agency to do the street ministry to tell us what was going on, because he felt that was a betrayal of pastoral confidence. We ended up having to fire him. That's when all the homophobia and name-calling and writing letters to the paper began to roll, where all institutions, especially religious ones, were perceived as bailing out, betraying, being hypocritical. I mean it all just rolled. It rolled.

Pam: For how long?

Well, in its raw intensity, right through that summer and into the fall. Out of that came a lot of recognitions. One was a commitment to combatting hate crimes; John Perry Ryan was involved in that. Another was confronting fear. The Meeting House, with Jennifer's predecessor, Kim Harvey, was really the only faith congregation that was anything other than fear-filled. All the other congregations circled the wagons and were testing the drinking water. I don't mean that literally, but, for example, we had to have discussions about whether or not a common chalice could be used.

Here at St. Mary's they didn't want to have a healing service, even though the Episcopal diocese was sponsoring healing services and had contacted St. Mary's the year before, quite appropriately, to have them. The vestry was so afraid of the contamination possibilities that they said no.

I said as soon as I got here, "We're going to have a healing service this summer and I'm not even going to ask you to vote on it, but I'll talk it out with you. You can tell me exactly how you feel. It can be grounds for the shortest tenure possible for a pastor."

Jeanne: What is a healing service?

It varies. Basically it's shaped in a way you'd recognize as a usual worship service. There's a lot of singing—especially hymns that speak of the human spirit being in touch with its depths: "There Is a Balm in Gilead," "Amazing Grace." Sometimes there are spiritual passages that have to do with, at least in the Christian context, the healing stories of Jesus; laying on of hands, prayers, lifting burdens, release; touching experiences, free spontaneous prayer, people talking out of their hearts about what it is like to be living with illness—either their own or a loved one's. In some instances healing oils are used—that is oils become the symbol of healing, or incense is used. It's eclectic, not specifically Episcopal.

Even though the healing service was theoretically in place when I arrived, we mainstreamed it, including the sacrament of healing as part of our Sunday morning service. All it needed was encouragement. People in the congregation were relieved; they could act out of their faith, their convictions of hope and affirmation, rather than out of fear. We had a number of people who signed up to go for training at the AIDS Support Group that first year. And we began to participate in helping to provide transportation, do shopping trips, become directly involved.

We also had the example of John Perry. This is not John Perry Ryan, but rather a man in this congregation, well advanced with AIDS. He was on the faculty at Harvard. He had come back to the town of his birth to live in his family home and to die. He came to church, sang in the choir, but because of the fear-filled reactions that summer of '88 he walked out of the congregation. The interim pastor who preceded me here in that fall of '88 began to visit John in his home. He told me how horrible these visits were as John just raged against the church. But he sat there, helping him get that rage out of his system. Completely, totally justifiable rage. He told me to call on John Perry.

He was very, very, very diminished by the disease. In February when I was to be installed as new pastor—we call it a celebration—John agreed to come and present the oils of healing. I can still cry at how ... his vision was impaired; he had to be helped by people standing at his side; but that grace that just lifts people to another place supported him. He stood there because he wanted something better for this place. He died that fall, was buried here [he nods to the outside garden] with full honors from this place. John's prodigal gift to us was the celebration of a ministry that identified the emergence of healing as a mainstream sacrament.

We're all a part of this little spit of land. Often what is said about Provincetown is that this is a community that knows how to care for its own. Most people derive their sense of spirituality out of the larger environment, not out of coming to a house of worship. In moments of real crisis all the contentiousness gets set aside; it doesn't disappear, it's just set aside. The need to pull together, to literally fight a fire that's blazing in a building, or help a neighbor who is thrown into crisis, is habitual. The community has responded to sea tragedies, the loss of fishermen, sailors for years and years; it's second nature. Foley House is a wonderful example of what I'm talking about. It was a total community effort. Two agencies, the housing authority, the PASG forming a partnership and going after the resources. Then there was that incredible moment when they tore the building down.

Pam: And that was just an error, wasn't it? Just a mistake?

That's what's been conjectured and we'll never know. I probably came as close to knowing as anyone. I went over to the Patrician [a local store] to get a newspaper the day the crew arrived to take down the parts that needed to be renovated. I remember thinking, "Wow, at last we're underway." Then Gordon called me saying, "Get over here, they're taking down the whole building," he was calling all the other board members, trying to stop the demolition. I went over with a couple of other people to show them and the whole thing was gone … gone. All the funding was based on this being a renovation project. But the board wouldn't quit and held the contractor completely responsible. He argued that it was cheaper to do new construction than to renovate, but they finally settled without going to court. That building is built and it's a magnificent structure. It may have arisen out of contentiousness, just as the history of the PASG was marked by contentiousness, but it held together, is going forward. That's kind of the way we do things here.

We're raising a granddaughter whom we've adopted. Jessica will be eleven this spring and the experience is additionally rich because she is the child of John, one of our adopted black children. Actually there is some Native American blood in John as well.

Through Jessica our sense of this community is heightened. I think most kids are remarkably open and welcoming. It's when adults act their worst that kids get thrown off balance. I suppose Provincetown kids get called things like "fag" at athletic events away from home; they have experiences where the diversity here is put in their faces in a negative way. But, for the most part, their experience of the gay community is that these are good neighbors; they care for each other; their businesses are great places to go. Firsthand experience is the prevailing experience, after all.

☙

Ed Frock

Logical, well-organized, patient, prepared—not many things in life ambush Ed Frock. He speaks with care, not caution, thinking through the implications of most questions before constructing his answers. It's difficult to imagine him in the aggressive fast-track dollar-driven world of the New York real estate boom in the '80s. Yet that was the job he had before being called to the ministry. Our conversation took place in his small, neatly arranged office in the basement of the Universalist Meeting House. Photos and memorabilia line the walls. One, immediately over his desk, is a color photograph of Ed looking at an AIDS quilt exhibition in Washington, DC—a figure dwarfed by the immense expanse of creatively stitched memorial patches.

☙ It was around the time of the real estate crash in 1988 that I started to question what I was doing for a number of reasons. I was encountering AIDS and HIV more and more in my life, realizing that this was something I could be vulnerable to. I started coming to terms with my own mortality. I remember reading Tolstoy's *The Death of Ivan Ilyich* and putting that together with the beginning of AIDS. I knew I had to leave New York City, and since I had spent several summers in Provincetown previously, I came here. This place has always been a spiritual home for me, a place of spiritual exploration.

Living here that summer of '89 was a quiet, meditative, reflective experience for me. I lived on the East End, didn't come into the town center a lot. I didn't take part in that summer madness. I also discovered the Meeting House and for the first time in my life experienced a woman minister, a congregation and a religious movement that accepted gay people. I started to revisit childhood ideas of wanting to be a minister.

While I was living here in the fall of '89, I took the HIV test for the first time. I took it because they were first starting to treat people who were asymptomatic; I could see a reason for knowing my status. So I tested, and I tested positive, as I expected to. It was still a lot to deal with at the time.

I got accepted at divinity school in '90. My first year in divinity school I worked as a hospital chaplain, but gradually I realized that I wanted to focus on helping the gay and lesbian community rediscover and explore their own spirituality.

Completely serendipitously I ended up working at Victory Program, which is an HIV and addiction agency; I worked in a halfway house with men in early recovery from addiction, many of whom were HIV infected, all of whom were at risk for HIV. That experience was the very kind of experience I wanted to acquire. I felt like I already had good exposure to the gay male experience of HIV and AIDS, but I needed and wanted to know more about the drug user's experience.

I ended up working two years there while I was in divinity school, and between those two years I worked as an intern minister in Rochester, New York. Shortly after I finished school, Victory Programs hired me to develop a volunteer buddy program for people with HIV who were also in recovery.

When Jennifer and I were in divinity school together we fantasized about being co-ministers of this church, even at a time when there was no possibility of that. After Jennifer started here and realized the magnitude of the need, she asked me if I would be interested in an AIDS ministry.

I had to sift through anxieties and concerns. Might it be too stressful for me, too intense? What were the boundaries? It was really during the interview with the committee who drafted the proposal for the AIDS ministry that I began to feel comfortable. They understood the importance of setting limits and they were willing to support me in taking care of myself. I felt like I couldn't walk away from it, that this was the place I was supposed to be.

Jeanne: You said you had always considered Provincetown a spiritual home. Was it because of the proximity to the sea, the landscape?

That's part of it. There is this physical beauty. But there's also a special kind of interaction among people that Provincetown fosters, one different than other places I've lived, like Boston or New York. There are opportunities to just "be together" with people, to know them more fully. I guess I consider that a spiritual experience.

People open up more. My understanding is that before Jennifer arrived here there was not a lot explicit acknowledgment of the magnitude of grief in this town. She really made it her mission to try to confront that, attend to it. With that process under way, a lot of doors open. For example, the night before Christmas eve I gathered with a few friends. We got together because we care about each other, but also because we wanted to talk about what it's like to go through Christmas without people we loved, people we'd shared holidays with in the past. It was a very, very powerful experience—gathering together as friends, as family really.

This is a town where people seem almost instinctively to

create rituals that purge and cleanse. Jay Critchley's Re-Rout-ers ceremony is an example, a ritual where people attach to a tree all those things they want to and need to release. Then they set the tree on fire and push it out to sea. It's incredibly powerful.

I feel like the support groups we've started are doing pretty much the same thing, not only releasing emotion, but developing a discourse about the emotional impact of living with HIV, the spiritual challenges of living with loss. People are intentionally creating the kind of community they want to be part of.

Pam: Isn't that new threshold of perception precisely what you were talking about in your New Year's "liminal sermon"?

Yes, yes it is. [He looks for a copy of the sermon. We read together these sections.]

"One way to understand the turning of the year is as a 'liminal' time. From the Latin word for 'threshold,' the noun *limen* and the adjective *liminal* describe a threshold of perception. The word *limit* also comes from the same Latin root. I understand a liminal space or a liminal time or a liminal experience as one that is associated with a limit or a boundary or an edge. But even more than that, a liminal experience is one that carries us to and perhaps even through a perceived threshold from one place or time or experience to another.

"By their very nature, liminal experiences possess a great power and potential for transformation, for they carry us to the edge that separates what is familiar from what is foreign; they carry us to the gateway between what we know and what we don't know.

"Worship is also a liminal experience, and the design of this building echoes and helps manifest that this is a liminal space. Coming to Sunday morning worship at the Meeting House, we exit the busy-ness of Commercial Street, entering first into a garden whose lush, quiet calm signals to us that we are leaving the realm of everyday business. The large front doors draw us inside, where, as we rise to the second floor, we shake off a bit of the dust of the outside world with each step. In the second-floor foyer, surrounded by relics of the history of this congregation, we are already aware that we have emerged into a separate and different kind of space. Finally, when we enter this sanctuary and settle into the cushioned pews, the soaring ceilings, the light flooding through the tall windows, the grand *trompe l'oeil* wall treatment, the beautiful mahogany woodwork, the Sandwich glass and chandelier the resonant tones of the pipe organ—all these sensual experiences of sight, smell, hearing, and touch—work together to communicate that here we have stepped outside of our everyday lives into a very different and special place and time.

"In the liminal space of this room, we find ourselves poised on a perceptual threshold, in a gateway between the material world and the world of the spirit. Here we may experience time or space differently. We may experience ourselves differently. We may experience our connections with other people and with the world around us differently. Here, from time to time, we may feel ourselves in touch with the world of the spirit, with the people we've cared about who are physically no longer with us. Here, from time to time, we may feel ourselves in touch with God.

"Or perhaps there are other liminal places for us where the veil between the known and the unknown, between the material and the spiritual, between the past, present and future, is rendered transparent. Last weekend I ran into an old boyfriend with whom I spent some magical times in Provincetown in the early 1980s but hadn't seen for years. As we caught up on each other's lives, he told me that whenever he engages in a guided meditation where he is instructed to picture himself in a very beautiful and special place, that place for him is Provincetown. I was fascinated to hear that because for me that place is a spot on the beach at Herring Cove, where I have also visualized myself saying good-bye to good friends who have died.

"For my friend, for me, and for many people, Provincetown itself is a liminal place. Here at the end of the world, Provincetown is not only a limit, an edge, the tip of the Cape. Throughout the years, Provincetown has been for countless numbers of people—all kinds of artists, writers, musicians, spiritual seekers, and general wash-ashores—magically, mystically, a threshold of creativity, a gateway to personal transformation.

"Provincetown is a liminal place precisely because it is both an edge and a gateway. Many of us who have made this place our home have done so because we have felt ourselves on the margins in other places, and that experience in itself has been a gateway to great learning and growth for us. For those of us committed to the life of this community, Provincetown—for all its foibles and flaws—is a place where we seek to create a community that defies conventional limits, a community of radical equality, a community founded in love and support, a community that leads the way in celebrating and accepting difference of all kinds.

"As some anonymous thinker has put it so eloquently, 'When we come to the edge of all that we know, one of two things will happen: either we will fall into the abyss or we will learn to fly.'" (*January 7, 1996*)

Edges, with all their peculiar sense of risk and exposure, have their own mythic appeal. Thrust thirty miles out into the sea, Provincetown's edges sharpen human perceptions. The ocean, a presence that dwarfs our own, confers scale. The unique sea-refracted "Cape light" triggers new ways of seeing. Perhaps, as Ed Frock suggests, edges create thresholds of awareness, ways of being together that defy conventional limits. If so, the Universalist Meeting House seems one such gateway, its light tower a beacon for those both literally and symbolically "lost at sea."

Chapter Three

Commercial Street

Eight-thirty A.M., September 7, 1996: Some flickering concern registers in the eyes of volunteers moving tables and setting up chairs for the Ninth Annual Swim for Life, an event designed to raise money for local AIDS service groups. Skies are clear, the water temperature in the 60s, but a stiff breeze blows directly into the Boatslip Beach throwing the water into high chop. A week earlier Hurricane Eduard dealt a glancing blow to Provincetown, and this weekend Fran is already ashore further south, sheeting the Eastern seaboard with torrential downpours.

Volunteers keep one eye on the sky while setting up their stations. Mark Finnen, organizer of the volunteers, sports a straw boater and calls out assignments to newcomers. John Perry Ryan neatly folds two hundred blue T-shirts commemorating the Swim, arranging them by size on a table. Irene Cramer tapes and marks clothing as swimmers exchange sweatsuits for wet suits. Irene Rabinowitz counts and numbers prizes to be awarded later in the day. All swimmers must have a minimum of a hundred dollars in pledges to register, but most arrive with considerably more than that. Some organizers were concerned since the PASG Arts Auction, held the previous weekend, raised $87,000 in the community and the Boston to New York AIDS Bikathon, an event drawing many of the same athletes, is also scheduled this weekend.

The indefatigable Jay Critchley, the Swim's founder and organizer, seems to appear in several places at once, the bouncing feather on his red Stetson weaving in and out of volunteers, swimmers, and public address systems.

By 9:30 a steady stream of swimmers crowds around the registration tables. Some, like John Tom, are veterans of the annual event and chat casually with friends. Others pace nervously, pulling on Poland Spring water bottles, smearing Vaseline on arms and shoulders, stretching out leg and thigh muscles. One newcomer admits that although he's trained daily for 6 months for the event, "it was always in a pool. This is different," he says to nobody in particular, eyeing the ocean, "this is very different."

By 10:30 the breeze converts to wind and the primary colors of the prayer ribbons dance wildly from the balcony railing. The streamers, each memorializing a loved one or representing a personal dedication from a swimmer or volunteer, are among the first things a swimmer will see when crossing the finish line.

Jay Critchley calls the crowd into a semblance of order, offering instructions on ferrying out to Long Point to begin the 1.4 mile course. When a rescue squad worker begins to describe the symptoms of hypothermia the crowd grows very still. Speed is less important than safety and all open water swimmers have a healthy respect for the ocean. The course will be lined by Coast Guard personnel and over thirty support and spotter boats, but as one veteran describes it, "Provincetown Harbor is a mean one, where you're usually swimming into chop. It's hard to see and it's easy to get fatigued."

Longtime Provincetown resident Ted Cass copes with the chop and lack of visibility by swimming the entire course on his back. "I've got the Long Point light house in view the whole swim and I take in a lot less salt water," he says, windmilling his arms.

The transport boats arrive to take the swimmers to Long Point. Some are tiny two- or three-passenger dinghies which can chug right up to shore; others are larger pleasure craft like the boat manned by

Mary Jo Avellar and her husband, which hovers 30 yards from shore while swimmers kick out and climb aboard. Quickly the boats are loaded and off, a convoy whose vanishing point is the lighthouse.

From shore the actual start of the event is difficult to distinguish, but once in the water the bright orange caps of the swimmers form a moving blanket rather like a slowly inflating life preserver thrown on the water.

Some of the best swimmers pull away from the pack quickly, and the life preserver converts from a horizontal to a vertical shape. Several sea kayaks begin their exacting work of monitoring swimmers for signs of fatigue or cramping. On shore the volunteers mobilize to prepare a welcome. Well-wishers, tourists, and simply the curious thicken at the front railing of the Boatslip deck, or walk in from Commercial Street to collect on the sandy shoreline. Those with bullhorns or operatic voices begin steady chants of encouragement. Cheerleaders cheer. Those skilled in drumming, surely every third resident of Provincetown, begin the steady cadence that accompanies many ritual occasions in the community. Drummers even hop aboard small boats so that their accelerating beat can be heard more clearly by swimmers.

In less than half an hour the leaders are clearly visible, caps veering around moored boats in the harbor, kick sprays distinguishable from the high chop in the water. Several volunteers like life-jacketed Gwen Bloomingdale and sequined Tim Burton wade out into the water shouting encouragement, pointing out the coordinates of the finish line to those slightly off course.

Now the crowd erupts into surround-sound: stomping, clapping, shouting, cheering, whistling. Many run down to the water's edge as if to personally carry the early finishers the last thirty yards. Some are in tears.

Karen Krahulik arrives to thunderous applause, followed quickly by Scott Robinson and Gus Baker. Their times are less vital than their temperatures, and blankets, towels, hot tea are quickly shuttled through lines of volunteers. Catherine Kroger of Brewster, a veteran ocean swimmer approaching her seventy-first birthday, completes her fourth swim. Big cheers go up when "the nieces" come ashore holding hands.

The four young women—three sisters and a cousin—who converged from Boston, Connecticut, New York State and Baltimore, swim for a community that they have visited since childhood and for a cause that is dear to them. Ted Cass backstrokes in. The crowd lingers beneath the rows of waving prayer ribbons.

Tim Burton, shivering in his Diana Ross outfit, wades further out into waist deep water encouraging swimmers, pulling them along with steady chants of encouragement. Through it all the crowd stays, punctuating each arrival with a chorus of congratulations. Back on deck, swimmers collect their clothes, their eyes registering elation and some small remnants of fear. John Quinn, a writer for the local newspaper *The Banner* and a first-time swimmer, articulates what many feel as they grapple with the fear that accompanies the Swim.

> I was more than 100 yards from the start at Long Point when I panicked. I felt a tightening in my chest, breathing was a challenge, and the harbor's buoyant, salty water turned to quicksand. I remembered that, before the Swim, I was warned that this sometimes happens to novices of the open water, that you should just try to backstroke your way through it. But in fight or flight mode, my instincts begged to know, where's the side of the pool? I seriously thought of swimming back to Long Point, but instead stripped off my snug fitting wet suit, which seemed to restrict my breathing, A new start I remember thinking.
>
> Then came the real reason I was able to finish the Swim. A solitary kayaker saw me waving my waterlogged suit and approached. In a kayak he was practically at sea level, almost a buddy in the water. I confided in the kayaker that I was nervous—"undertrained mentally, though not physically," is how I think I put it at first. Then I strategized. "If you stay with me," I began to bargain, "just please stay near me," I lapsed into begging, "I think I'll be able to do it."
>
> Only when we spoke after the Swim did this kayaker, Marc, tell me that he heard fear in my voice.

And so I had a companion. At the time, I didn't even think that I might be selfish, restricting his availability to rescue others. A few times I looked up and didn't see him and immediately called out "Marc, where are you?" like a blind man temporarily stripped of his watch dog. "I just need to have you in my sight when I turn to breathe. Promise you won't go," I said.

He didn't, and together we finished. It took me over an hour. The Swim takes it toll on even the most elite athlete, but battling fear and anxiety nearly depleted my resources. I think fear stayed a steady stroke or two behind me, or was neck and neck with me, but on the other side of Marc's kayak, so I didn't always see it.

As we neared the finish line at The Boatslip, I was no longer looking for the big blue landmark. Then I saw Marc's outstretched gloved hand and I heard him say, "John, you can stand now."

Marc the kayaker, I learned later, is Marc Paige, a long-time summer and steady off-season resident of Provincetown. Marc told me how wonderful the experience was for him. He said he felt very needed, that he experienced as great a sense of accomplishment as the swimmers. He said he felt in partnership with me.

Marc also told me he has AIDS. Early this summer, Marc was told the disease was at an "advanced" stage, but in June he began new medication which has improved his condition. Enough that he could row his kayak across the harbor, even if he can't even think of swimming the course.

Marc refers to his disease as his "disability."

"Fear can disable, too," I told him.

"But you learn to live with it, or in spite of it," he said.

I hope we both do.

☙

The Swim for Life is one measure of how Provincetown lives "in community," how it yokes private goals to a common purpose. Some interpret "For Life" pragmatically: they swim to raise money for local AIDS service groups, for the alternative therapies necessary to prolong life. A passion for the open water, a commitment to the environment spurs others. Some, like John Tom, "dedicate the Swim to those who have done it in the past but have died, and to those who want to do it but are unable." Jay Critchley has been there from the beginning, the Swim's founder and yearly organizer, a maypole around which many definitions of community dance, around which many private and public rituals revolve.

Jay Critchley

Jay Critchley is a lanky Puck escaped from a rehearsal of A *Midsummer Night's Dream* into a post-flower-child world. While there are many things worth being serious about, nothing is solemn in Critchley's world—or if it aspires to solemnity, he'll prod it gently, insistently, with mischievousness.

Tall, agile, carrying authority lightly, it is as easy to imagine Jay in a business suit as in his Re-Router's get-up—a flowing full-length ball gown constructed entirely from plastic tampon applicators, accessorized with a Viking helmet topped with giant lobster claws.

Jay enjoys the absurd in the same ways the French absurdist playwrights did. Pushing the edges of the envelope by creating projects and performance art like the "Immaculate Protection Condom Company" and the "Blessed Virgin Rubber Goddess," his intention is to tease out meaning from meaninglessness, to find the sacred in the profane, to lift icons out of institutionalized settings, to shock, dismay, provoke, stimulate.

His creativity extends beyond outré art exhibits and ritual dress-up occasions. He has contributed his organizational talents to the Family Tree Project, a living memorial of trees planted on public land in memory of those who have died of AIDS in Provincetown, and to the Art Archives, a collection of paintings, sculptures, letters, photographs,

costumes, videos, preserved to honor the memory of artists who have
lived and worked in Provincetown and who have died of AIDS. Currently he is working with the Provincetown school board on a magnet
school project, one that will draw upon the diverse resources and heri-
tage of the community to offer students an extraordinary educational
opportunity. In the old-fashioned sense of the phrase, Jay Critchley is
a "solid citizen," even, or perhaps *especially*, when he has his lobster
claw helmet at ready.

       I arrived here in 1975, moving in part because my wife's fam-
ily was here. I think the environment, the sheer beauty of it,
attracted us. Prior to that I had been doing mostly human
service work: I was a Vista volunteer in Oregon, I worked in
Connecticut in drug rehab programs, and then here in Provincetown I worked for five years at the Drop-In Center, a peer-
counseling program mostly addressing young people's needs
and those of their families. Within a year after arriving here,
my son was born, I came out as a gay man, and then eventually I came out as a visual artist. That whole process was difficult for me. I was angry. I didn't like it, I didn't want to be it.
Dealing with my sexuality occurred when I was twenty-nine,
and it was not until I was thirty-three that I became an artist;
that identity was buried even deeper than being gay.

Pam: How did that process occur?

I was totally engrossed with creative things when I was young.
I come from a family of nine kids, Catholic schools, colleges,
church almost every day, rosary everyday. I'm an "Irish twin"—
that's a sibling born in the same calendar year. So I spent lots
of time collecting things, making things, holed up in my room
making Christmas presents, Halloween costumes for all my
relatives and family.

     I spent quite a few summers on an incredible little island
with my aunt, uncle, and cousins—off of Niantic; there I collected shells and made things for them. Now I collect other

things. [Laughter. Jay's "found art" consists of projects and pre-
sentations constructed from condoms, tampon applicators, tires,
driftwood, claws and fish bones, feathers.] I was going through
a long process of identifying myself as an artist; the layers were
being peeled off slowly.

Pam: Was Provincetown an integrated community, gay and straight working together, in 1975?

Yes and no. I think up until ACT-UP there was a sort of
generalized agreement that everybody got along, liked each
other. When ACT-UP decided to march in Provincetown for
two consecutive summers, the town just came apart. Lots of
questions about community, about standards, about censor-
ship emerged from those marches: Who defines what the community is? Who belongs here and who doesn't? Who determines the standards of a community?

You have to imagine the spectacle of the marches: AIDS
activists, Dykes on Bikes, Rollerina. Do you know Rollerina?
[He gets out a photo of a tall bewigged figure wearing Rollerblades and an outfit somewhere between a tutu and a ball
gown.] She was well-known in the '80s, a stockbroker in New
York, who showed up for such parades on her rollerblades and
dressed in her gown. She led the parade. A lot of people were
outraged by ACT-UP, wanting to pretend that the trouble-
makers were "radicals from New York," not "*our* gay people." I
think the marches unearthed some of the simmering resentments and conflicts that did exist here, but that had never
been acknowledged before.

Pam: Was there something that aided the healing process, or did the
debate just subside?

The conflict played itself out over the next few years. There
was the famous Spiritus conflict. [Spiritus is a popular pizza
shop on the West End.] In a nutshell Spiritus became a central
symbol of conflict in the town. A lot of people go there after

the bars close, large crowds which block the street. So there were several ugly confrontations, turf wars actually, circling around the same issues: Who owns the community? Who determines what laws are being broken? Whose "rights" are being violated?

And of course beneath gay and straight conflicts lie economic and political issues. That's the key. During the real estate boom in the '80s a lot of townspeople sold their property to lesbians and gay men and moved to the suburbs, to Truro. They sold their houses for high prices. Lots of the Portuguese population left. And what are you left with? Monied gay people who are property owners, who have political power.

Now I think we're facing here what may be a unique situation in this country, where gays will become the "majority" rather than the "minority" in a town. We need to stop thinking of ourselves as victims and to begin thinking about how to organize power better, how to honor the minority rights of the straight people, the Portuguese people, the children who live in this community. We need to be very conscious about including other voices in all the decisions that affect our community. Surely gays understand that better than most.

Pam: Tell us how you started the Swim for Life.

Well, I'm a swimmer—a daily swimmer in the harbor during the summer. One day when I was swimming in the harbor right at the Boatslip Beach with my friend Walter, we looked at each other and said, "Do you think we could make it across the harbor?" We got a boat and someone who would follow us, and we made it over to Long Point.

Initially, I think we conceived of doing the Swim as an environmental celebration. That was the summer of '88 when a lot of New England beaches were being closed because syringes and waste were being washed ashore. Provincetown never had a problem like that since it has the highest tide change on Cape Cod, a nine- to eleven-foot difference between low tide and high tide. Imagine the flushing out of the harbor with that huge volume of water and energy. Once we thought about the symbolism of purification, we connected the Swim to AIDS. The first year we had sixteen swimmers and made $7,000. Now the event takes up to 150 volunteers to run, draws several hundred swimmers and nets $70–75,000. The thing that makes the event exciting, really engaging, is that so many people swim who don't think of themselves as swimmers. Some people take it as a personal challenge, as a way to deal with their grief. One person, actually a roommate of mine one summer, couldn't swim at all at the beginning of the summer and made the Swim by September. People with HIV, people with AIDS have done the Swim. At least fifty percent of the people who swim are just determined that they'll participate, that they'll finish. There's energy and healing in this process and also the release of a lot of grief.

Jeanne: Have you lost a lot of friends to AIDS?

I can't keep track of them all. After thirty people I stopped counting, and that was seven or eight years ago. Now I want to start counting again because I am afraid of forgetting. This whole community is in mourning.

You can't ignore your history here. Your experiences accumulate and ultimately you are responsible for who you are, who you become. You can't hide, you can't escape, because if you have a problem with someone—chances are you'll see that someone almost every day. So you and others get to know yourself in your fullness as a human being. You really have to want to be here. There's one road in and one road out, and it's probably one of the few places on earth where almost everyone who is here has consciously *chosen* to live here.

Pam: How do you take care of yourself after all those losses?

Well, I do my Re-Routers Ritual every year, a ceremony that brings together all of the elements that are vital to me: the artist, the performer, the ritual, the community, the harbor, the attack on the awful consumer consumption of Christmas. I feel like I get much more out of it than I put in.

I'm sure ritual has always been therapeutic for me since I was a little boy washing the feet of priests, lighting votive candles, chanting. And I'm equally sure that acknowledging loss is an important component of dealing with grief. This is a community that has always experienced loss. One of the strongest images that comes to my mind when I focus on Provincetown is the image of a woman waiting on the beach for boats to return, waiting as a witness to determine if her husband is dead or alive. If I were ever to do a Provincetown memorial—a narrative one like the one in Gloucester—it would be of a woman standing on the shore looking out to sea. That image captures the whole interaction between the human community and the natural environment and it's ageless. In a way, we're all waiting to see what life brings. We're all witnesses.

ॐ

Irene Rabinowitz

This year the Swim for Life also benefits HOW [Helping Our Women], an organization helping women who are facing chronic or life-threatening illness. Irene Rabinowitz, a Selectwoman and former volunteer at PASG, has been a central organizer of HOW. She met with us at the HOW office on Commercial Street to describe her experiences in a variety of capacities during her nine-year tenure in Provincetown: as an early volunteer at PASG, a Selectwoman during the "Spiritus incident," and most recently a staff employee at HOW.

The HOW office, a small neatly arranged resource center and meeting room, is tucked into a tiny mews just off Commercial Street. Outfitted with a wheelchair, respiratory equipment, and several large shelf units crammed with books, brochures and informational pamphlets, the office is both welcoming and utilitarian. Irene took a call just as we arrived, offered some advice and a phone number to the caller, and then turned her full attention to the interview.

Clearly her previous experience working in personnel for several large New York corporations has produced the wide range of organizational skills so desperately needed in small grass roots organizations like PASG and HOW. She excels at a variety of tasks: grant writing, number crunching, advocacy work, outreach work—and she approaches all of these tasks with deep wells of energy. A woman of warmth and easy humor, she can also instantly switch into an "all-business" attitude. She speaks with the rapid-fire delivery of someone accustomed to covering a lot of territory before lunch; occasionally mid-sentence she pauses and laughs—as if to say, "What's the rush?"

    I'm a New England native; I grew up in Rhode Island and then lived and worked in New York for sixteen years—first at ABC and then for Colgate-Palmolive. When the pace and consumption of that atmosphere grew intolerable, I left and went to work for Fortune Society, a grant-funded organization doing outreach work for prisoners—alternative sentencing, advocacy work, direct services for men and women coming out of prison. Eventually, I knew I just had to get out of New York. I loved Provincetown, a place I'd been coming to all my life, and I wanted to be closer to my mother in Providence. So I ended up here, where I wanted to be, surrounded by water.

    This isn't a life you'd choose if you're a capitalist: I make much less money than I did twenty years ago. It's a completely different way of life, a different set of values. My move was a spiritual revolution too, probably something that you've heard from other people, and I also wanted to write more, which I found impossible in New York.

Jeanne: What kind of writing do you do?

    I've been taping and writing up interviews with Holocaust survivors from one particular section of Poland. It's a project I've been working on, on and off, since 1983. Many of the people are gone now, so it's important to keep at it, contact people who are still alive. I also write a column for *Province-town Magazine* which helps pay the bills.

When I first came to town, that very snowy winter of '87, I met Jay Critchley, and he and I opened up a retail store for a while—a whale watch store. As I got more oriented I also volunteered at the AIDS Support Group. Although it had been in existence for a number of years, it had no real staff. Alice Foley, Preston Babbitt, George LeBone, Paul Ramos—all were sort of operating out of Alice's car and Preston's guest house. I can imagine what some people must have thought when they checked in to Preston's elegant Victorian guest house and stumbled over six cases of condoms. When I came they had done one volunteer training session and I was in the second volunteer training program.

Pam: How quickly after you started did you get into grant writing, or on to the staff?

It took a while, since there really was no staff. The grant that actually paid for the first staff positions was written by Alice, Preston, and my ex-husband. I typed it on my old Selectric, but they were the ones who wrote it. I was there for more than six years, gradually converting from volunteer to staff member, case management worker mostly.

I also was appointed to the town Finance Committee and later was elected as a town selectman, a position I've held for six years. I had only been on the board a few months when there was a riot at Spiritus. Probably it wasn't billed as "a riot," but that's exactly what it was.

Pam: A gay/straight riot?

I'm not sure what it was. It was a drag queen riot, basically. A drag queen had a plunger and stupidly stuck it on a van. The police officers, instead of going over and saying, "What are you doing?", pulled their police car into the middle of the huge crowd, put him in the back, and then tried to pull out. The crowd—pretty drunk by then, it was 1 A.M.—wouldn't let them leave. I got a call to go down and by the time I got there it had turned ugly: people throwing things, rocking the car. The police handled the situation as best they could, finally walking the person to the police station while the crowd trashed the car. The whole incident landed on CNN and got big coverage in the *New York Times*. And that incident spawned a lot of intense board meetings with heated discussions about "special rights" for members of our community. And from all of this emerged some good legislation—protecting people, all people, from hate crimes of any sort: racial, religious, sexual. It spurred some re-examinations of Provincetown as a community.

Jeanne: Tell us about HOW: how did it get started?

A group of women got together in 1992 and began to explore ways of gathering information, support, and services for women with life-threatening illness. We formed an organization to create a resource center where information would be available on alternative therapies, nutrition, support services. Later we started to provide direct services for a woman with cancer and a woman who had a stroke. Now we provide transportation, some stipends for women who are eligible; we have some volunteers who do companionship and family respite work. We have a support group for women with chronic illness and a support group for women with HIV.

Pam: If I were HIV infected and wanted services from PASG, would I be able to do it?

Yes, yes you would. We share clients. There's no female case manager there, but, on the other hand, when I worked at PASG I had all male clients. I think the communication lines are open. If you look at the whole spectrum of women's health issues, however, HIV will be at the bottom of the list. There are many women in this community who have had strokes, cancer, multiple sclerosis. But there's shame attached to a sexually transmitted or drug-related disease. We're at that stage with HIV and women in this community. It's a stage that will pass. Remember when we were kids everybody whispered the word *cancer*?

Jeanne: You mentioned earlier that you experienced a spiritual "revolution" when you came here. Is that process still going on for you?

Oh, yes. When Douglas [Brooks] came to the Support Group he and I would talk about how these spiritual issues needed to be addressed, but we seemed at that point to be the only people talking about it. Now with Ed [Frock] and Jennifer's [Justice] work, the spiritual dimension of all health issues is becoming more central. George Welles is just a gift to this community, and my community of faith, Am HaYam, is vital to me. There's a small spiritual coalition that also includes a Methodist minister and a Catholic priest working to do things in a less traditional religious way and a more open-ended spiritual way.

I must say though that we're a community of 3,500 and sometimes I feel like only a small nucleus of people serves on the front lines. Usually it's the same people whether they're tackling health issues, or human services, or spiritual awareness.

Perhaps the work I've done around the Holocaust and the work I've done with people in the criminal justice system keeps things in perspective. I think that I'm steeled to expect that people are going to behave badly nine-tenths of the time. That's my defense. When they behave well, when the earth seems populated by real human beings, then I'm nicely surprised. I'm always willing to be surprised.

かわ

Mary Jo Avellar

Mary Jo Avellar, a native of Provincetown, is especially well positioned to describe Provincetown's community values. With the exception of her college years and short periods of time living in Hawaii and
California, she has lived in Provincetown all of her fifty years—a span
permitting perspective on changes the town has experienced: the changing profile of the Portuguese community (she is half Portuguese), the
loss of the fishing industry, the rise of tourism, the loss of affordable
housing. She was chair of the Board of Selectmen when ACT-UP was
at its peak. She and her husband, Duane Steele, owned the Red Inn, a
popular restaurant in the West End, until two arson fires forced them
to sell it. They also own and operate *The Advocate,* the oldest of the
two weekly newspapers in Provincetown. Mary Jo speaks with the
quiet authority of someone who has absorbed Provincetown's rhythms
for a long time and with the incisive edge of the good reporter that she
is. A woman of composure and professional demeanor, she broke into
tears while describing the intensity of "one terrible year" when she lost
five very close friends to AIDS. The arc of her Provincetown memory
is both wide and concentrated, and her experience as a journalist gives
her the capacity to function as an observer and participant simultaneously.

    Well, the winters I remember here as a child were very similar
to the way they are now: lots of snow, not very much going on,
hardly anyplace open to eat, people getting by on very little.
The demographics have changed, however. For example, in
my high school graduating class, the class of '64, there were
fifty-two kids; there are only twenty-two kids in the junior class
today. There are obviously many fewer children, many more single
people, old people, than in the Provincetown of my childhood.

    Once I graduated I was encouraged to leave by virtually
everybody. Unless you married right out of high school and
stayed, it was sort of understood that to be successful you had
to get out of town.

Pam: You moved away to attend college?

Yes, I went to UMass in Amherst and then, upon graduation in '68, left with my best friend to live in Hawaii. I came back four years later, actually going to California for a while. But I missed the Cape a lot. I was very homesick for Provincetown, which seems to me to be a place like no other. I'm a real snob about it. I have no desire to live outside New England.

Pam: What neighborhood did you grow up in?

We grew up in that neighborhood down near Ciro and Sal's where Harvey Dodd has his studio shop. My father was born and raised just down the street from there, where originally he had waterfront property. He rented small boats for a time, and later he sold the little boatyard and bought the schooner. Do you know the one I mean? The beautiful wooden one that took folks on harbor cruises? He loved that boat and owned it until he was eighty years old. He was always on the water, all of his life. He didn't like to fish commercially, but during the war he was a Boston Harbor pilot; Boston is where he met my mother. Even though she was a regular summer resident here, they met in Boston. My cousin started the Dolphin Fleet of whale watching boats, so we've always been associated with the sea. The Avellars are synonymous with the sea.

Jeanne: What changes have you seen in the neighborhoods?

Oh, there are so many. Of course there was the huge real-estate boom of the '80s with all the condos. Property grew very expensive and most rentals were converted into condos. The Portuguese community sold off a lot of its property. So I think it's much harder to live here year round.

People have tried, are trying, to halt unbridled development. The conservation people are scared. People are upset in the arts community because of a lack of affordable housing and studio space. There are all the problems with water and

septic systems that overbuilding creates. I suppose the real-
estate boom here isn't too much different from the boom anyplace else—except here it takes place in a three-mile area.

Jeanne: To what extent has the invasion of the AIDS epidemic affected
the town?

There isn't a person in town who hasn't been affected by AIDS.
Not one. And in one way or another the whole community
has responded. Even teenagers, kids who sometimes have difficulty with some of the more overt displays of sexual behavior
among the young summer crowd of gay men, the cavorting
after the tea dances ... that sort of thing. Even those kids raise
money for AIDS support. This past weekend, eight kids walked
seven and a half miles and raised $1,500, half of which they
gave to PASG. Some high school kids cooked dinner at the
Support Group the other night. So even though during the
ACT-UP period the town was accused of being homophobic,
I think there's lots of evidence to the contrary.

Jeanne: You were here during ACT-UP?

I was the Chairman of the Board of Selectmen. I think in town,
at the governmental level, we were really afraid that there was
going to be an ugly incident. We had a lot of police in town
the night of the parade. And the kind of incident we feared
didn't occur—certainly not of the magnitude of the ACT-UP
incident at St. Patrick's Cathedral, for example. But the parade was so offensive to most people I knew, gay and straight,
because we felt that the accusations were unfair, unfounded. I
don't think many people would object to demonstrations—
lots of them grew up in the '60s, after all, and thought of
demonstrations as pretty routine. It was the anger, the rage,
that offended people, and the fact that that anger was misdi-
rected, or at least that's what many of us felt. Provincetown *had*
responded to AIDS, just as it always has taken care of its own.

I think it's hard to understand just how people cope with

the effects of AIDS. In one terrible year, for example, my husband and I lost five people—all concentrated within a four- or five-month period. We just lost all our friends. [Pause] It was awful. Awful.

Douglas Brooks asked Duane and me to read names at the Vigil Memorial Service. We appreciated the invitation. [Long pause] But it was hard.

In order to put all this in context you have to understand small towns, how they operate, what to look for. For example, you may have the most intolerant person in Provincetown. Maybe he hates all gay people—but *not* the one who lives next door to him. This guy is going to take care of his neighbor. It's always been that way: neighbor helping neighbor.

The rescue squad and the EMTs are wonderful, they're wonderful. And more recently the town has come forward with alternative therapies and health care. Acupuncture, massage therapy, herbalism—it's almost like a cottage industry.

When you think of the courage of Alice Foley and Preston Babbitt, how they came to the Selectmen's meeting one night and told us of their idea to start something to take care of people who were sick, then you grasp what was and is remarkable about this community. Alice was an avenging angel—out there on the front lines for AIDS. She took on everybody to get the funding.

You know everyone has responded in one way or another, tried to contribute to the ongoing AIDS fight. I think back to when my husband and I owned the Red Inn. A series of very difficult things happened. We had two arson fires; the bottom fell out of the stock market, so financing was tough; we had the newspaper to sustain, too. We figured we had to sell the restaurant, move it out from under our control. One of the things we thought of was a hospice for people with AIDS. So far as we knew no housing for people with AIDS was available, and here was this big, spacious building, on the water, in a beautiful quiet spot on the West End. So we approached Walter Boyd who was president of the Support Group at the time, but they couldn't handle our request. Still, things have a way of working out; now Foley House exists.

This is a tough town to live in and if people don't help each other they're just not going to make it through the winter. That was true before AIDS and it's true today. Part of what defines Provincetown as a community is necessity. And part of it is the resilience of the human spirit.

✍

Lenny Alberts and David Matias

Necessity and human resilience help define Lenny Alberts and David Matias. Dr. Len Alberts is a physician who left a Boston practice in general surgery and a faculty post at Harvard Medical School to come to Provincetown in 1986. He works as the Director of HIV Services at the Outer Cape Health Services. His life partner, David Matias, a former actor and theater director and currently a poet, was a 1994–95 Writing Fellow at the Provincetown Fine Arts Work Center who also co-chaired the committee for the AIDS ministry at the UU Church. David was diagnosed HIV+ on his twenty-fifth birthday, eleven years ago.

The interview, scheduled in late June, not long after David was released from the hospital after proton-beam radiation, took place at their home. Their Commercial Street home, at the very tip of the East End, looks out over the bay. The white sands of Truro, backlighted by the sunset, are visible from large picture windows in the living room. Two gray cats, a brother and sister team named Booda and Opal, presided over the occasion. Among the topics discussed was the recently announced resignation of Ed Frock, AIDS minister at the Meeting House.

Since each partner helps define the values and life work of the other, it seems appropriate that this conversation is a duet—two quite distinct voices which gain resonance and complexity when heard together.

🐟 **Lenny:** Previously I was involved in academic medicine, practicing for roughly seven years in Cambridge and on the faculty of Harvard Medical School. I decided to leave and travel for about six months in Australia and New Zealand. When I returned, there was a position available at Outer Cape Health Services. So I put some stuff in storage, rented out my Boston apartment, and came down. The story is a little more complex, but that would be my book, not your book. Here I am ten years later.

David: I was aware even growing up in the hill country of Texas, the son of a minister, that I was gay. I decided the way out was to focus on good grades, concentrate on the arts, go to college. And that's what I did. Slowly I came out in college, first trusting and telling my sister, and then waiting for readiness in my mom and dad. This was the early '80s, and even though I had a great job, a car, an apartment, something just wasn't right. Then I got the shingles. I went through hell for weeks. At one point I looked like John Merrick, I was so swollen with blisters. Deep in my heart I wondered, "Is this AIDS?" But then I recovered, and back then, if you recovered from something, then you reasoned it must not be AIDS. When I scheduled a follow-up appointment, the doctor tested me without counsel or permission. Basically he said, "You have about a year to live," and gave me the card of an immunologist. The day I found out was my twenty-fifth birthday party. My sister knew, so as soon as the party was over we just went into the bathroom and cried and cried. We decided that we had to do better than this, we had to find a way to grow, to be strong.

When the opportunity presented itself I got into graduate school at the University of North Dakota in theater, got my M.A. in '88. I was asymptomatic at the time and, instead of moving to New York, moved here to Provincetown in 1988. Lenny had a room he was renting in the house and I met him first as a landlord.

Pam: How did you get involved with the UU Church?

> **David:** At first I thought I'd like no more church, please. I wasn't an atheist, but an agnostic. But then I heard Kim Harvey's sermons and I realized that here's where I can recover some of that lost spirituality.
>
> **Lenny:** Well, when I moved here I realized I was embarking, to some degree, on a spiritual quest. Certainly the thought of fulfilling any aspect of that through organized religion, anything that smacked of Christianity, was not part of my agenda.
>
> But after the first summer here, after Labor Day when things began to slow down a bit, I went a couple of times and heard Kim Harvey, who was really quite captivating. I'm not sure exactly how it happened but Kim and I became personal friends. We would get together and have lunch a couple of times a month, let our hair down, knowing full well we were going to maintain each other's confidences totally.
>
> At that point I didn't have many long-term patients; I was basically a walk-in or episodic care provider at the clinic. So I decided to hit the road again, this time going to Nepal thinking I'd make more of a commitment to Third World medicine. I realized quickly enough that my skills weren't needed in Nepal. Without sanitation, without clean water, without electricity, without vaccinations, without hospitals, without drugs, there was little that I could do. I discovered that I did need to be a healer, but that my training and experience and mentality were Western. Born a Jew with 6,000 years of Judeo-Christian heritage behind me, I discovered you can be a Buddhist for a day, but you are what you are.
>
> I was getting letters from Provincetown saying "When are you coming back?" The need was here. Gradually more and more people were infected. So I came back and signed a contract. Interestingly, two months later David showed up. My "enlightenment" was going back home, doing what I do best.

Pam: You talk about the spiritual quest that brought you both here, yet you define it differently.

> **Lenny:** Yes. For me it's staying open to something that transcends the mundane, whether it's spoken by a Unitarian minister, a patient of mine on his deathbed, or within a poem of David's. David was more in touch with his spiritual capacities than anybody I'd ever been with before.
>
> **David:** I felt my bond with Lenny grow and grow, but I also felt confusion and tremendous guilt. Why would he want to get involved with somebody with AIDS? That's all he does all day.
>
> Since I had been asymptomatic and hadn't trusted any doctors since that first one, I re-tested. When that came back positive I started at Outer Cape Health with my first AIDS doctor, Donna Cooper. They did everything: blood tests, appointments, counseling, and when she said, "Is there anything else you need?" my whole guilt and confusion about Lenny spilled out. "Listen," she said, "I'm your doctor, he's your boyfriend. Let him be there for you emotionally. I'll be there for you as a doctor."

Pam: Have you been able to do that?

> **David:** It's a difficult line, but when she said that I just broke down. I thought I was going to be a major burden to him.
>
> **Lenny:** There are never any guarantees in life or in medicine. I had one of my HIV patients die of a heart attack. David and I just celebrated our eighth anniversary. Would I rather have him HIV negative? If that were the case, he probably wouldn't have come to Provincetown in the first place. He would have been in New York on stage, or waiting on tables wishing he was on stage.

Pam: David, you were instrumental in Ed Frock's hiring for the AIDS ministry. Now he's leaving. Will you be involved again in helping locate a replacement for him?

> **David:** It's too early to say now. Originally, the goal of the Futures Committee was to create a foundation for the AIDS ministry, to mold it. We got some money—one of the biggest grants available, plus the Bicycle Fundraiser, which generates money and enthusiasm. It's in place, it won't dissolve, and Ed did much to ensure that. He established two support groups, he raised money. We knew his status from the start and tried to build in health days and vacations.
>
> **Lenny:** But he also ran into a lot of needy people who said, "What, you're going to Boston yet another Friday? You're not here today?" Chronic illness can make people needy, and there are a lot of needy people in this town, both inside and outside the church. Perhaps Ed is trying to come to terms with his own needs, his own system of beliefs.
>
> What would it be like for me as a doc treating HIV fifty percent of the time if I too were HIV+? I think it would be sort of like a second-year medical student reading about a disease and then discovering his own symptoms, turning the page and reading about another he's also sure he has. When I see someone lying on his deathbed it's hard enough for me to say, "My God, I can't imagine that being David," But I never get to the point of saying, "My God, I can't imagine that being Lenny." Ed didn't have that luxury. Ed held himself to a high standard. Hopefully, he'll be better for having done the job and for having drawn the necessary limits.
>
> **David:** I like the word *boundaries* more than *limits*. In such a small town it's very difficult to respect boundaries.
>
> **Lenny:** I understand that completely. For example, I see fifteen to twenty patients a day; I'm the senior doc at the clinic now. The last thing I want to do is go to church and see thirty or forty of my patients there. It's like a big waiting room. It's

not a place of serenity for me, although I have great respect for
Jennifer Justice.

Pam: Can you tell me a bit about the new coalition between Outer
Cape, Deaconess, and Beth Israel hospitals?

> **Lenny:** Well, I'll try to make this relatively short; it's of great
> benefit to the AIDS community. Cape Cod Hospital was clearly
> not a place that AIDS patients wanted to go for treatment. At
> the same time, Deaconess was opening an AIDS unit, where I
> helped train some of the docs. There was a problem, however,
> since the unit felt AIDS patients needed to be treated by a
> specialist, so if Outer Cape patients were referred to Deaconess
> their medical records stayed there. The docs at Outer Cape didn't
> have the medical histories of Deaconess patients. Beth Israel,
> a better AIDS hospital, absorbed Deaconess; the docs at Outer
> Cape were given staff privileges at Beth Israel, and computer-
> ized medical files were available to all the docs. This works
> much better, in part because AIDS patients at Beth Israel are
> treated with greater sensitivity and respect.
>
> **David:** I'm a good example of that. My first hospitalization
> was in the summer of '91 at Deaconess. They put me in this
> huge room, no one else around. Everyone wore gloves, used
> paper plates. Lenny and I, in our dark humor way, began to
> joke, supposing that AIDS activism for equal treatment had
> gone too far.
>
> This hospital stay, nobody had any trouble coming near
> me, I was in a small room with two other patients. Now we
> joked about the good old days in isolation.

Pam: Obviously you've both lost friends since you've been here?

> **David:** There have been so many for me lately that I wrote a
> poem about being unable to erase them from my address book.
> I'm not going to erase their names; my address book has be-
> come a memorial.
>
> **Lenny:** There are three tiers of people that I've lost: some of

my oldest friends when I was first coming out in the '70s, some of my first boyfriends, most of my contemporaries. There's just an overwhelming sense of sadness that pervades my life. One of my closest friends, a guy who shares my birthday, died four or five years ago. We used to have joint birthday parties. I still wait for him to call on my birthday.

Pam: You were a doctor in the clinic when ACT-UP did the "die-in," weren't you? What was your take on that?

Lenny: Well, our administrator was more upset than I was, although I was pretty upset. To put it in context for you, people were dying left and right of Pneumocystis pneumonia; no one knew what to do. All of a sudden there was some evidence that Pentamidine, which had been an orphan drug from the '50s, was effective in an aerosol fashion. In the beginning, Bactrim or a sulfa drug was also effective, but paradoxically, a lot of people with HIV couldn't tolerate sulfa. So the Community Health Center [now Outer Cape Health Services] started administering aerosol Pentamidine, even though it wasn't approved by the state or approved by Medicaid. Those were the kinds of things that could put a clinic license in jeopardy. We had one patient who needed Pentamidine. He was getting it in Boston and we made sure that, if he wasn't able to go to Boston or needed it on the QT, we would give him Pentamidine. Our administrator didn't want to go public with this information until the Department of Public health okayed it. In *sub rosa* fashion, however, we were making sure nobody was going to die of Pneumocystis.

I was acting director and I guess ACT-UP's "die-in" was the moment when I realized that health issues were the easiest way to politicize other agendas. I agree with ACT-UP's tactics and deeper agenda, but I don't feel we were the enemy.

There were several people participating in the "die-in"— John Perry Ryan, who is a very thoughtful, politically sophisticated activist, and some others who wouldn't know a T-cell from a T-bar lift. I felt I had to take the brunt of a certain amount of misplaced anger. But John and I ... well, I know where he's coming from and he knows where I'm coming from. He lost his partner.

Pam: We heard about the new drugs, the protease inhibitors, recently. What can you tell us about them?

> **Lenny:** Well, there is tremendous excitement, of course, when any new hope appears on the horizon. Ten years ago that hope lay with AZT [retrovir]. But the virus is highly mutable and quickly became resistant to the effects of AZT. Protease inhibitors allow for the invention of what is known as a triple combination therapy, often referred to as the "AIDS cocktails." Thus far they seem to be effective in suppressing the virus and decreasing AIDS deaths. But today's facts may be Monday's fiction. AIDS deaths still account for the most common cause of death for people between the ages of twenty-five and forty-four. Further, the cost of the new drugs is very high. For example, an annual dosage of saquinavir [Invirase] can cost $4,300, while the cost of ritonavir [Norvir] can creep as high as $6,750. You have to also remember that while the protease inhibitors hold out real hope for some, others whose immune systems are already too compromised can't withstand the myriad of side effects produced by the use of the multiple drugs. (Long, long pause)

Pam: David, originally you were involved in the theater, and is it primarily poems that you write now?

> **David:** I wrote plays all through college and yet could never be entirely happy with that form. Theater is the art of compromise—a team effort. I've always written poetry. I did continue to do some theater after moving to Provincetown, but after I directed Who's Afraid of Virginia Woolf?—losing 10 pounds in the process—Lenny cautioned me to stop.
> I applied to the Fine Arts Work Center, despite the fact

that "locals never get it" and five hundred people apply for four positions. On the third try they gave me the fellowship. That was a kind of validation.

I think I'm more of a prose poet. I try to listen to language, select phrases that strike me. Then the thing evolves, kind of like a puzzle you put together. For example, I wrote a Passover poem triggered from the image I had as a child about the blood over the doors of the Jewish people that would cause the Angel of Death to pass over. I started to work on that image—what happens if the Angel of Death comes and there's no blood on your door. And then Lenny told me a story about his father, one thing followed another, and it all came together.

PASSOVER VERSE
You took me to my first Seder.
Short & 84, your mother had no
trouble setting up her dining room.
Milky porcelain plates, on dull white linen,
holding the egg, shank bone of lamb,

bitter herbs, welcomed us to a ritual,
telling me more about you
than the religion. As she placed
the yellow-brown *charoseth*
made with the nuts & apples,

you looked out the kitchen window
mumbling a complaint about
your father's *damn* orchard.
Rotten fruit smashed all over the lawn.
His dream of a beautiful garden

buried with him over twenty years ago.
You hate when she romanticizes that weedy
backyard. The marriage to her was ripe,
full of love—not a reflection of the bruised mess
the sourness you stare at upon the unkempt grass.

Your solution, *Tear them down.*
She mumbles (the way you do)
Oh, we mustn't, your father loved those trees.
You remember otherwise, as a child
recalling their ugly fights over them.

With bobby-pinned satin *yarmulkes,*
food-stained paper books of *haggadahs*
at the elbow-cramped table,
The Four Questions were recited.
I'm not the youngest,

so I asked my own to myself:
How often is this man on your mind?
What if your father had known we were gay?
Would he have passed us the four cups of wine?
Would he have handed us the holy *matza?*

After I spoke the last line in my section:
God delivered us from slavery to freedom,
from darkness to light, all your relatives,
years of hearing monotone,
gave my dramatic flair an ovation.

You can't imagine your father smiling,
clapping, patting my back ...
We went up the old carpeted stairs to your
mother's shy room and you went somewhere else,
glancing at that photo of Emmanuel

on Miami Beach in a black bathing suit.
You shook your head ... disappointed ...
I'm beginning to look just like him.
You can see that, though you can't see him,
the way your mother sees him.

The crime rate in Hartford is so high
when she wants to visit the grave on his *Yahrzeit,*
she must arrange for a police escort.
You asked aloud, *Is this love or duty?*
Your mother hugged me, kissed me at Passover.

She knew I had AIDS. She introduced me
as your "good friend." I am your good friend,
not your "wife." I can forgive those sins of shame;
like when my mother lied to a friend who
pestered her about why I wasn't married.

He's chronically ill and didn't want to put
a woman who loved him through all that.
I was angry at Mom, like you get with yours,
because I do have a spouse
and you are going "through all that."

When our mothers call us long-distance
shocked at the death of some elderly aunt,
we remain patient in the midst of this pandemic
watching the young die continually.
We understand our mothers' anxiety, we all know it.

There's no blood on our door and the Angel is coming.
We love the earth so much we don't want to leave it.
They realize they're older and all the more alone.
Like our friends, they are closer to death,
scared without the presence of the familiar.

And so we can forgive, a chance you never had
with your father; he died the day before
you graduated from medical school.
He doesn't know me, he doesn't know us ...
would he accept our union if he lived today?

You said he followed the Jewish ceremonies
only because your mother forced him. Remember,
my love, he wanted to see apple trees blossom,
to taste what grew on his land, to fill his mouth
with the life of Spring—sweet and alive.

On December 13, 1996, several months after we conducted this interview, David Matias died; thirty-five years old, he had lived gracefully
and courageously with AIDS for nearly ten years.

Despite the simmering resentments that bubbled and occasionally boiled
in the late '80s and early '90s, Provincetown has always sought to
define itself as a place of partnerships, a place that grapples with what
it means to live "in community," a place where sometimes in the
deepest water—as John Quinn discovered—the "disabled" save the
"abled."

Chapter Four

The Breakwater

At the very end of Commercial Street just before the great salt marsh opens out into the Province Lands, a long curving causeway of boulders stretches out, a connecting pathway to Wood End. From there a sandy spit stretches out to Long Point Light, Provincetown's farthest promontory. These cross-layered stones withstand the rush and withdrawal of tidal waters, a twice daily torrent of broad water washing and washing the harbor.

Walking out on the Breakwater requires some dexterity; massive boulders of different heights crisscrossed by crevices and the deep pock marks of erosion test any casual stroller's balance. Gulls dive-bomb the causeway, dropping their cargo of clams and mussels on the granite surfaces—a deft exercise in de-shelling. A half-mile out to sea a stiff breeze flattens the diminishing marsh grasses and all but the determined turn back to shore. Away from the bustle of Commercial Street the sounds of the sea begin to insist: whip and lap, gulls' plaintive cries, rhythmic surge and withdrawal. A listener develops different antennae, receptors tuned to elemental cold salt water frequencies.

At Long Point, where a fog bell tolls warnings, the cradle that is Provincetown emerges. Here the peculiar geology of the "outermost reach" is strikingly apparent. Born of the drift and deposit, the glacial

Cape ends at High Head in North Truro. Provincetown and the Province Lands are post-glacial, a giant sandbar composed of material carried north by ocean currents and winds, gradually forming the bent arm of the harbor. In geologic time the sandbar is very young, perhaps five or six thousand years; its existence as a peninsula will be brief. Someday the sea will tear the coastline apart and what was once continuous land mass will become a series of shoals and islands. This is the place John Hay called "the first and last land in America."

To walk on the Breakwater is to feel the tenuousness of all human effort, the abiding fluidity and alteration that underlies this barrier of stones, the brevity of this sandbar. What is it in the human spirit that constructs a Breakwater, that curious oxymoron of strength and permeability? What messages can we translate from these inchoate rocks, this man-made barrier reaching out to Wood End and Long Point Lights?

≈

There are several ways of making a stand. John Perry Ryan's activism via ACT-UP and the formation of the Provincetown Positive Coalition is one way of drawing a visible line in the sand. The therapeutic practices of Janice Walk and Katina Rodis suggest another kind of Breakwater, a consciously constructed therapeutic conduit to those struggling with HIV/AIDS. Kelly Kelman's one-on-one experience as an AIDS "buddy" is yet another causeway, an intimate bridge to the life and death of another human being.

John Perry Ryan

John Perry Ryan—a name invoked in several previous interviews as the organizer of ACT-UP demonstrations, a founder of the Provincetown Positive Coalition which broke with PASG, and a force behind Provincetown's hate crimes legislation—resembles a younger version of the actor, Richard Dreyfus. He has the same moral earnestness and disarming smile as Dreyfus. Equipped with an unusual capacity for recall and chronology, Ryan pieced together the events that precipitated his activism. Perhaps hindsight coats anger with logic, since beneath the chronological structure of his narrative, frustration surfaced and dove. Ryan believes that expressing anger is intrinsically healing, a belief that casts light on the history of ACT-UP and its appearance in Provincetown. As he talked about its co-founders in Provincetown, Erik Kendrick and Paul deRenzis, it became clear that ACT-UP's mission—forcing a governmental response to the AIDS crisis, forcing AIDS into a commanding position on the national agenda—became increasingly urgent in the years of 1988, 1989, and 1990. Challenging priorities, challenging the lack of access to "experimental" or alternative therapies, challenging indifference or ineptitude, exploring avenues for self-empowerment—all describe not simply the mission of ACT-UP or the Provincetown Positive Coalition, but also the personal credo of John Perry Ryan. As formidable as his advocacy has been, Ryan is a reflective man, one who sat curled in a modified lotus position in the armchair of our motel room as he recalled and resignified the events leading to his activism.

I moved to Provincetown in 1987 with my lover, Keith Andrew Donahue. From the moment we arrived he was sick. We didn't know what was wrong, bad flu, something like that. He was sleeping twenty-three hours a day.

Around Thanksgiving, he started having some problems with his eyes. We went up to Deaconess on Thanksgiving Eve assuming he'd be admitted. They looked at his eyes and decided they weren't going to admit Keith, so we drove all the way back, stopping at Stop and Shop at 10 P.M. on the way back trying to locate some semblance of a turkey for an impromptu Thanksgiving dinner.

The day before Christmas he was admitted to Mass General with a presumptive diagnosis of CMV Retinitis. I came back home, returned Christmas day, then came back to get somebody to look after the dog so I could return and stay with him as long as needed. He called me the day after Christmas and said, "My vision is going and I can't get anybody to do anything about it." He called every hour saying it was worse, he could see less and less, and finally at 4:30 P.M. he called and said it was gone, totally gone. Keith was an artist. He had lost his vision. It turned out to be not CMV Retinitis but something called Atypical Retina Necrosis, which just destroys your retina in a matter of months. They told him this was not HIV-related. Sent him home and he got sick again, an upper-respiratory infection that turned out to be Pneumocystis Pneumonia. Back he went into another terrifying ordeal.

We had some Provincetown friends who had medical connections in New York, people who started the Community Research Initiative of New York and who were using aerolized Pentamidine to treat Pneumocystis Pneumonia. We went to New York with a hundred dollars, all we had, and when we walked into the office we found a lot of men in various parts of the office doing the inhalation therapy which is standard now. It was a sight to see. The drug, of course, wasn't licensed for that purpose yet. After taking an extensive history of Keith, the doctor agreed to give him his first treatment the next day. We said we didn't have the money and he told us not to worry, to return; Keith had his first treatment. The doctor gave us enough Pentamidine for ten treatments as well as what he was using to create air pressure to force the Pentamidine into a mist, an asthma machine. He asked us to go back to Keith's doctor with a letter from him detailing how to administer it and how to get Medicaid or health insurance to pay for it. You call it Pentamidine Therapy, and it is the second line of treatment for Pneumocystis after Bactrim fails. We were absolutely elated at the possibility of preventing people with AIDS from dying from Pneumocystis—the number one AIDS killer at that time. But neither Donna Cooper at Outer Cape Health Services or Alice Foley gave us any support. I think they felt that since the drug was as yet unapproved they'd risk losing their licenses.

So Keith and I started a guerrilla clinic in our house. The New York doctor continued to supply us and we did it in our home. All the time we tried to persuade Outer Cape Health Services of the practicality of doing this. Others in New York and San Francisco were doing it and nobody was yanking a license. They were cautious at best. So we started the PWA Coalition in May of 1988, which eventually became the Provincetown Positive People with AIDS Coalition to provide information and self-empowerment.

Pam: How did you see that organization as distinguished from PASG?

It evolved as a source of information about alternative and complementary therapies for people with AIDS. We were radical in that we were trying to buck the death sentence, trying to develop survival strategies until there was a cure.

The excellent work of the AIDS Support Group had in it all the pitfalls of AIDS service organizations elsewhere: the creation of dependency relationships for clients, no consumer input. We wanted some complement to simply taking care of people who are preparing to die. But that idea prompted so much resistance that it erupted into a political battle. Oddly enough, the Provincetown Positive PWA Coalition is now housed within the offices of the AIDS Support Group.

Pam: How long did Keith live?

He had a very short life after his diagnosis. He was diagnosed in January of '88 and died the following December. Probably he had been positive for a long time. For a very long time I was … numb. I couldn't remember what his voice sounded like or what he looked like unless I looked at a picture. [Long pause]

Pam: What was your involvement with ACT-UP?

In August of '88 we organized an ACT-UP demonstration at Outer Cape Health Services around the aerolized Pentamidine. We did a "die-in," a two-minute demonstration that I think was heard around the Cape, around Boston, because it was covered in the *Boston Globe*. About forty people walked in, held up watches. Some people with AIDS had written on their backs "Time is Running Out"; others held up signs saying "Aerolized Pentamidine Now." We lay down on the floor like we were dead. You could almost hear a pin drop. It was very moving, almost surreal. Then they called the cops. For a long time after that I was ostracized; in such a small community it's hard to take on some of the people in power and not make enemies.

Pam: What's it been like more recently for you in the town? Are you still active with ACT-UP?

Yes, oh yes. With both ACT-UP and the PWA Coalition. I'm the director of the PWA Coalition and it's an enormously different climate now. We're looking at some of the issues around women's exclusion, what we need to grapple with, take responsibility for. Women with AIDS still feel like they have to hide in Provincetown.

For me personally, I guess I really feel numb to a lot of the sadness. I rarely cry, but when I do I can't stop crying. Almost all of my initial circle of friends are dead now. I'm HIV negative, and even though I don't like the distinctions now that have developed between the positives and the negatives, I feel an enormous responsibility. Enormous. Not only to fight for social justice—but to fight for a cure.

If not here, where?
If not now, when?
If not us, who? —ACT-UP

Janice Walk

Janice Walk, a Provincetown resident for twenty-three years, has the directness of one who has made a "fearless inventory." Early in the conversation that took place in her home she volunteered that she has been "in recovery for fifteen years" and that that seminal experience has informed many of her life choices, including her decision to become a therapist. She deals with many AIDS clients in her practice and has run both HIV negative and HIV+ groups at PASG. Her warmth and self-possession make it easy to understand why volunteers and staff at PASG mention her repeatedly as a rudder, as one who guides by example.

The well stoked wood-burning stove in her living room was welcome relief from fierce winter weather. We had spent the morning unfreezing the pipes in our crow's nest with a hair dryer. Janice joked about her early days in Provincetown when she rented a cabin "whose pipes froze if the temperature dipped below twenty degrees." Tall, resourceful, quick to laugh, she had the toughness to work in a methadone clinic and the insight to identify the chinks in her own armor.

      ℞   I came here first in the summer of '71, loved the beauty and magic of the place. The next year I went back to college to finish my B.A. in Art and History and decided to move here permanently in May of '73. I'm an artist and the light and color here are unique.

         When I first got here I cooked in restaurants and lived on unemployment in the winter. Twenty years ago it was a very, very cheap place to live. At that time there wasn't such a thing as a "condo." It was just wonderful old houses with Portuguese apartments in them: no closets, no insulation in the walls, wallpaper that had seahorses on it. Really great stuff like that. The gentrification of the town came much later.

Pam: When did you get your social work degree?

         I went to Boston University in 1988. I went two years full-time, got my degree and then worked at Boston City Hospital in the methadone clinic for two and a half years in order to do my supervision time

That was really an amazing job, since there you probably saw a much truer representation of what urban AIDS looks like: equally divided between men and women, lots of children who came to the clinic with infected parents, lots of infected pregnant women. I supervised and ran the pregnant addicts' group. I also worked with the IV clinic. Liz Brown was doing a lot of research on pediatric AIDS at that time and she was part of our team.

The clinic served a very large population; four hundred people a day came in for methadone. We dealt with a lot of people with HIV and AIDS who were homeless; their primary method of transmission was IV drug use. Every horrible situation you can think of, we had. My goal was to get my LICSW and come back to Provincetown to practice and work with the Provincetown AIDS Support Group. The contrast between what is possible to do in an urban setting and what is possible to do here is enormous.

Pam: Why?

Well, the sheer numbers dictate that some people in urban areas will simply fall through the cracks. And many people have a difficult time getting the services they're entitled to because they can't decipher the system. They miss appointments, they don't do the paperwork. A lot of energy in cities is spent on outreach. Here in Provincetown you can focus on direct services.

Granted there are a lot of people in Provincetown who have a hard time admitting that they have HIV/AIDS, so they stay away from services. Sometimes they have a hard time accepting entitlement benefits. They've always worked, they don't believe they should be "on the dole." They don't want to lose their independence. I think this kind of resistance is something we need to address more. Rather than faulting the people, we need to better understand the motives behind their reluctance.

Pam: Do you run groups at PASG?

Right now I'm running an HIV-negative gay men's group. I was running a PWA [People with AIDS] group for about two and a half years; I just took a break from that last summer. Running the PWA group involved working with five to eight men at a time. They'd die pretty fast, so the composition of the group was always changing. The group dynamic is a complicated one. People worry about a member's sickness, both in terms of whether their illness will mimic his, and in terms of losing another person they've grown close to. A lot of guys in the People with AIDS group are very lonely. They want to be connected to other people, but they dread getting close to somebody and then losing them in a matter of months or a year. When people who have lost two circles of friends attempt to bond, the whole dynamic is different. I lost about sixteen to twenty guys in that two-and-a-half-year period. We have to learn to cope with the repeated loss, with how it breaks the continuity of growth.

Pam: What are the issues in the HIV-negative group: survivor guilt?

Yes, survivor guilt is a big one. Everybody else got infected, why didn't I? Issues around safe sex, or "I'm sick of safe sex, why not just get infected since everybody else is?" Who wants to be the last man standing at Herring Cove Beach? Depression, anger, substance abuse. But lots of them are sober and have been for a number of years.

Pam: Do they struggle with that?

The people who are well into their sobriety don't. People who have been sober a couple of years sometimes slip, or sometimes vacillate—use once just to escape. Some people with anxiety disorders have to get tested repeatedly. And some who display the same degree of anxiety, refuse to be tested. I try to root out the fear factors for the people who are struggling with whether to be tested or not, and then support them in whatever decision sits right with them. I don't have any particular agenda on testing. I do have my own opinions about safe sex, about transmitting the virus or getting it.

Pam: How about your own private caseload?

Here we have a system underwritten by the Ryan White Fund providing four emergency sessions of mental health care for people who have HIV or are affected by it. I take a lot of those referrals, and have carried twelve or thirteen people with AIDS on my caseload. I asked for a break from that about the same time I asked for a break from the AIDS group.

Pam: How many other mental health workers are there here?

Right now we have more than ever. We have a psychologist, a counselor who is a masters-level person with years of experience. We have a man from Boston who is an LICSW who works here one day a week, there's another masters level counselor and a social worker all working with AIDS. It used to be basically three of us.

And then there's the work, very vital work, with volunteers at PASG. I've done pieces of the training: crisis work, substance abuse, empathic listening. Often volunteers are the only people who see housebound clients face-to-face frequently. They can detect substance abuse or pick up clues about suicidality. Sometimes they are the primary caregivers.

Pam: It sounds like a very full plate.

Well, this is a community that has always been supportive. The business people in Provincetown consistently donate money, food, services. Their efforts go on and on. I remember some years back that, at some level, I myself must have been denying the seriousness of this epidemic, how it, too, goes on and on and on. One day I was working in my perennial garden and tears just started running down my face. I stood up. I knew it was here to stay.

☙

Katina Rodis

Katina Rodis is one of the mental health workers Janice refers to as part of the Provincetown team. A psychologist, she's lived in Provincetown for eleven years, a move precipitated by her own battle with systemic lupus. She runs an AIDS therapy group which, over the course of four years, has demonstrated a remarkable degree of bonding, and which became the subject of a well-received video documentary called *Shooting Stars*, released in 1994. At the time of this interview, she had recently undergone a hip replacement and was using a cane; that fact instilled little caution in her year-old Bouvier, who jumped, licked, pawed, and exuberantly welcomed visitors to the house.

Much of her work with HIV/AIDS clients requires her to balance the "wake up call" AIDS issues to the infected and affected versus the deaf ear of the rest of America.

☙ I had to stop working for a period of three years because of lupus; I decided if I had to live on disability I could move wherever I wanted to be, so I moved from upstate New York to Provincetown eleven years ago. Even though I'm a psychologist I didn't think I'd be able to work. But in a year of so, at the urging of the minister at the Unitarian church, I began seeing clients. Since I've been working nine years now, half of my clients have died—all of them from AIDS.

About five years ago I went to the Support Group and said, "Look, I think group therapy would be a good modality to try here." They were open to the idea, so in the first year we tried an open group for eight weeks, giving people the option at the end of six weeks to sign up for twelve weeks. Eventually we got a core of people who were really committed to working together. So I approached the Support Group again and said, "How about if we try this one group as a closed therapy group and see what we can do with it?" We did, and, in its current form, I've been doing it for four years.

Pam: How has working affected your own health?

That's an interesting question. Lupus is a disease that's hard to predict. You know it's an autoimmune disease. It comes and goes. It's worse and it's better. I've had two hip replacements, actually on the same hip, and each time I have surgery I have a difficult time, ending up with infections. That's fairly typical of people with lupus. Working with people who have a different kind of immune disease also helps pierce my own denial. We are both confronting challenges.

Pam: How do you fight your own anger or despair?

If AIDS were a disease which primarily affected straight white men who make between $50,000 and $150,000 a year, there is no way on earth that there would not be more of everything: more treatment, more resources, more money, more research. There isn't a major hospital in this country that wouldn't have money for research. I believe that with every fiber in my being. That's hard to accept.

AIDS affects me in another way: I find it increasingly difficult to leave Provincetown. My partner and our two daughters live in Cambridge (Massachusetts); one of the children is learning disabled and needs the school system there. But that's a world that is very hard for me to be in. People don't talk about AIDS, nobody is losing friends like we are; I'm literally living in a different world than they are. Here AIDS is just part of our landscape. My partner and I try to bridge the worlds by visiting one another every other weekend, and the kids are here for the holidays and summers. It's not totally integrated, but it's as integrated as it's going to be.

Pam: Is it difficult to have a life where you're dealing constantly with the dying process and simultaneously a life where you're dealing with a seven- and a nine-year-old?

> That's what helps me keep myself together. Actually there are a lot of correspondences between the two. There are people I'm dealing with who are ill, are doing so much self-exploration, so much discovery—emotional, spiritual, mental—that they're growing constantly. They may be dying too, but they're growing. Right up to the point where they die, they grow. That's the process you feel with the kids—growth, discovery, self-exploration.

Pam: What triggers this self-growth process in the HIV/AIDS clients? Is it that belief about people growing stronger "in the broken places," people who know they are going to die wanting an enhanced life?

> That's the glib answer. I suppose a crisis will either elevate people or not. A lot of people have allowed the AIDS crisis to elevate them physically and spiritually. People who, before their diagnosis, drink and do drugs, decide after their diagnosis that they really want to live fully right up to the moment they die. Maybe they've always wanted to paint, so they paint. Maybe they've always wanted to write, so they write. They decide to extract everything they can out of life. Their diagnosis just seems to fire them up. I think when anyone is faced with death it puts us in touch with our life force.

Pam: What changes have you seen in the way services are provided here?

> The AIDS Support Group has grown more focused and the Health Services has also done a lot of liaison work with Beth Israel and Deaconess. That didn't exist before. Initially people were responding to crisis, and when you're responding to crisis, it's like fire management. You put out the first fire. You run over here and put out the next one. And the next. When you

get figured out, "we're gonna have those fires all year, and next year, and next year"—then responses get better organized, lines of communication open up. For example, the EMTs and ambulance people have grown to be amazing, just phenomenal.

Pam: How?

They're mostly heterosexual people who respond to people with AIDS in a completely professional way. They're also kind and thoughtful and respectful. They do their best. That's pretty rare in any setting.

Additionally, we have ministers in this community who reach out to help people in crisis. And the whole community reaches out to support the Swim for Life or PASG Auction.

But I'd be remiss if I didn't admit that living in the midst of constant crisis is abnormal, is devastating. To see someone who is spiritually evolving die—and die a terrible death—is, for me, personally devastating. This disease has eyes. If a person's a writer, he's gonna get Dementia; if a person's an artist, he's bound to get Retinitis; if a person's totally handsome, he'll get Kaposi's all over his face. It's very painful.

Pam: How do you take care of yourself?

The kids, the dog, I write. I have a garden. Sometimes I go and just look at the water. Yesterday Janice and I did just that. We went out to Herring Cove during our lunch hour and watched the seals. And people surround me with the art they've created. [She points to the walls of her living room and hallway which are covered with the paintings and artwork of her clients.] I'm circled by these wonderful reminders. [We examine some paintings together, a charcoal drawing, a small clay figure.]

Pam: How can you continue to do this work?

How can I not?

✍

Kelly Kelman

Kelly Kelman is an artist, creating flowered glass plaques, boxes, and pendants using flowers native to the area. She sells her artwork to local shops and at crafts fairs, and has worked as an AIDS volunteer in a variety of capacities. Her house where the interview took place was still decorated for the Christmas holidays, and the huge gas heater— which she referred to as a "Portuguese fireplace"—was humming. Quick to joke, especially at her own expense, she seems to use humor as a life-buoy when negotiating the deep waters of AIDS.

She brought out one of her glass plaques, tiny delicate flowers arranged in a mini-shoreline, a miniature of Provincetown. As she focused on her relationship with Mark, the AIDS client she befriended and cared for during the last six months of his life, it was clear that the experience was the best of times and the worst of times, a defining microcosm of love.

I came from Connecticut in 1970. At that time I was working as a research assistant in neurosurgery at Yale. There, although it was close to the water, nobody cared. Nobody ever looks at the water in New Haven; nobody knows if the moon is full, or if it's high tide or low tide. I had too many years of academe, too many windowless labs. I came here and suddenly I saw sunrises, sunsets, fishermen, little Portuguese women chatting away. It was no contest.

At first I worked in restaurants—cooking, doing dishes. But in 1975 I started making a craft item that went very well, and what I thought was going to be a hobby turned out to be my business. This is my twentieth year and I now make several items constructed of dried flowers in clear glass, leaded. They're done in landscape scenes composed of all the local things I pick here. So I make a little microcosm of what you see everyday.

Pam: How did you get involved with PASG?

I was slow starting that. This is my sixth year. I think for a while I was afraid of death and dying, and then I just grew angry. So many were dying. Gone. I needed to take some action, and so I became a volunteer with the PASG thinking, "Well, at least I can bring a meal. I can at least drive somebody to the dentist." I even thought for a time that I should go back into research.

After I joined the volunteers at PASG I did a little bit of everything. Well, not everything. I get lost so easily so we all thought it was better if I didn't take a group of sick people to Boston in the van. [Laughter.] But I did local Cape driving, and then I became a "buddy."

Pam: What's it like being a "buddy?"

[A long silence and an audible sigh]

It's a strange position. You're not a lover. You're not family. You start as a kind of mediator and then it grows and grows. What you're doing basically is committing yourself to an incredibly intimate relationship, to be with somebody until they die. You become a witness to and an integral part of their dying process.

Pam: Is Mark the one you sat with for a long time?

For six months. This is Mark. [She shows several pictures.] When people are dying, all the priorities get put in some order. You may be the one who hears things they've never told anyone, or the dreams they've never shared. Neither Mark nor I had had experience with the buddy system before, so we decided that we'd make it up as we went along, with guidance from Alice Foley.

At first, we just talked about lots of things and I quickly learned that confidentiality and consistency were most important. We'd check in with each other twice a week. We'd play

Bingo on Monday nights, that sort of thing.

When he started getting sick he decided, even though he came from a large loving family, that he didn't want to leave town. He chose Hospice and asked me to be his primary care person. Then came all the conflict at PASG, the battles between the leadership and the consumers, and despite the fact that he was very weak, nauseous from chemo, Mark became a voice of dignity and truth for the consumers, the voice that said, "This is what we need to do and I have nothing to lose here." I don't mean to sound dramatic; he was just telling the truth as he saw it. We ended up both resigning from the Support Group at that point.

Then from January through June I was with him daily. His parents would come on weekends, but I would still check in for a couple of hours. Often I would wake him up in the morning at 10 and put him to sleep at night at 11:30. Spend twelve to fourteen hours a day. By this time our closeness was beyond a friendship; he was a soulmate.

He had lost thirty pounds, and was living on grapes, watermelon and Gatorade. He had Kaposi's bad on his leg. It was black from his upper thigh to his toes. But Mark was Mark. He was a vegetarian and he'd say things like "Let's go get a big fat steak at the Patio Bar." Or he'd say, "This is May. I was supposed to die in February." Even Hospice said, "You probably don't have more than a few weeks." And I'd say, "I think you're redefining the word *linger*." [Laughter.]

Once after he grew self-conscious about his therapist coming over twice a week for months, he said, "Katina is going to be here in fifteen minutes. Just throw a towel over my head and pretend I'm dead." There was humor and love and caring right to the end.

When people enter their dying process they don't care how much money they've earned or what positions they've held. They talk about who they loved and who loved them, how they left their little mark on the world.

꧁꧂

We walk the Breakwater out to Wood End to glimpse the site of the "S-4 incident." It is a January day with high seas and narrow bands of gray cirrus clouds, perhaps a day not unlike the day of the accident. On a December afternoon, a Saturday in 1927, an event happened off Wood End that still haunts the consciousness of Provincetown: a Navy submarine, the S-4, in a bizarre accident, was rammed and sunk, taking the lives of forty men.

On the day of the accident, unaware that the Navy was conducting submerged deep water trials in Provincetown Harbor, the Coast Guard destroyer *Paulding* came across the bay from Boston to sweep the area for rum runners. Storm warnings were also flying, making conditions even more difficult. The *Paulding* steamed straight into the submarine's testing grounds. The S-4 was just beginning to emerge from a practice dive when the speeding destroyer struck her. Provincetown, toughened by many years of wrecks, now stood by to witness a terrible horror. Slow suffocation 110 feet below the surface went on for four days while divers struggled to save six men with whom they could exchange messages tapping on the hull in international code.

The *Falcon*, the Navy's only salvage ship, sailed from New London, and special divers Eadie, Carr, and Michels were dispatched from Newport, but no one arrived prior to 7 A.M. the next morning. Meanwhile, Boatswain Gracie of the Wood End Coast Guard Station went out in high seas for twelve hours on his surfboat, finding the submarine with his grapnel and losing her again.

Divers Eadie, Carr, and Michels went down repeatedly the next day trying to hook air lines into the submerged hull, but high seas and misplaced connections made their efforts futile. The Falcon decided to wait out the storm in the harbor, and on Wednesday morning, when diving was possible again, the Falcon discovered that the single buoyline attached to the sub was lost. Another grapnel was lowered. At this point Provincetown fishermen offered to help, suggesting that they could line up their flounder draggers and save time locating the wreck. The Navy refused their offer. That afternoon a line finally was made fast and the air line attached to the crew compartment. Only then was fresh air pumped into the compartment where six men lay dead.

In her classic *Time and the Town: A Provincetown Chronicle*, Mary Heaton Vorse describes the torment of Provincetown's residents who stood on the shore, all too well acquainted with sea tragedies. "People were crying in every house. They identified their own men with the men on the submarine. Why haven't they [the Navy] done anything? We'd save these men with our own hands ... Meantime, the weakening messages imploring help came from the men on the submarine. The town had become the center of the whole world. Town Hall had been made into headquarters for the press. Relatives of the men had come to Provincetown. The days dragged on ... Everyone in Provincetown had a feeling that it was their individual task to save these men and no one could do anything."

She concludes, "Provincetown never forgets the S-4. There is a special terror in the memory of those men waiting, tapping their patient messages, and dying."

In describing the agony of waiting, Vorse provides an historic frame for Provincetown's activism, for its determination to develop the muscle necessary for collective work. Fifty-five years after the dying men on the S-4 sent out their message, the AIDS epidemic hit Provincetown with recognizable force. This time nobody waited for the Navy.

Chapter Five

Hatches Harbor/ Herring Cove

Finding Hatches Harbor requires patience and no small measure of hiking stamina. Friends report simply "it's between Herring Cove and Race Point," or "it's where you watch the seals," or more pointedly, "take the fire road off Province Lands Road; you have to walk in a couple of miles." Even with the concentrated map that is the Province Lands, these are uncertain coordinates, for Province Lands Road is peppered with fire roads and their look-alikes: bike path accesses, logging roads, picnic pull-offs.

We prowl along the road in late afternoon, hoping to catch at least some glimpse of the fabled sunset at Herring Cove Beach. Although it is late March, skifts of snow still glaze the sand and collect at bases of the pines. On the third pass the proper pull-off materializes, a narrow slightly elevated road chained at its neck. Bayberry bushes and scrub pines thick with perfectly rounded brown cones mark the first half mile. The macadam bike path intersects the road, at first paralleling it, then snaking away towards the dunes. Gradually the landscape grows less domesticated. Stiff winds gather force over a long stretch of lowlands and the great salt marsh inlet, wild and lonely as a scene out of Sir Walter Scott, opens out toward the sea. Camphor smells of pitch and pine give way to bog and peat, to the trace odors of rusted tin cups left at outdoor springs.

The tide is out, so we drop down from the narrow dike that bridges the deepest sections of the marsh into the basin itself. Held in place by waving grasses and sea lavender, the gritty surface glints with shards of shells, bits of green and blue bottle glass. We leave no footprints.

The ocean's edge is rimmed by high dunes, hard to climb in the yielding sand. Atop one, we glimpse our first expanse of gleaming sea stretching out, out to where water and sky meet at a vanishing point almost indistinguishable by the human eye. We're too late for the sunset, but not for its afterglow—long streaks of pink and mauve and violet that suddenly authenticate all the glossy "Cape Light" photographs displayed on Commercial Street.

✿

Mark Doty has caught the particular poignancy of a Provincetown tidal salt marsh: "It feels inexhaustible to me, in all the contradictions which it yokes so gracefully within its own being. It is both austere and lush, wet and dry, constant and ceaselessly changing, secretive and open ... At low tide it's entirely dry, a Sahara of patterned sand and the tough green knots of sea lavender ... As the tide mounts twice a day, this desert disappears beneath a flood. It's a continuous apocalypse; Sahara becomes sea becomes sand again, in a theater of furious mutability."

Oppositions abound at Hatches Harbor and adjacent Herring Cove Beach. The salt marsh with its tidal plenitude and privation mimics in its natural rhythms the Biblical adage that "what is given" is also "taken away." The gorgeous sunsets at Herring Cove provide the theatrical scrim for spotting whales in the early summer, or seals in the dead of winter. A favorite spot for lovers in all seasons, it is also gilded with the ashes of a hundred memorials.

The stories that follow speak to the necessity of exploring the mutable ground that lies between sickness and health, between oneself and others, between chaos and receptivity. They point to the terrifying and yet strange, comforting recognition that we are all "replaceable and irreplaceable at once" (Doty), that we wish to leave footprints even in the face of the incoming tide.

John Culver

John Culver comprehends the "theater of furious mutability" better than most. An artist and craftsman who is currently a nursing student at Cape Cod Community College, John has lost two lovers to AIDS. Loss has made him more supple, more able to cross and recross borders between his own HIV-negative status and the diagnosis that so many of his loved ones have received. Perhaps it is appropriate that he supports himself by making glass kaleidoscopes, since he sees the world in a series of startling configurations, some beautiful, some strange, but none incapable of translation. Equipped with a surprisingly gravelly Louis Armstrong voice, John is thoughtful, philosophic even, about his life history, frequently using personal experience as a lens on AIDS, on gay culture, on survivor consciousness.

    I came to Provincetown in 1982, stayed the first winter. In April I got sober, which is where I met Bill, who was also in the Program. About a month later I moved in with him in Wellfleet. We were together for eight years until he died of AIDS in 1990.

    I do glass work, kaleidoscopes, which I still wholesale today as my main source of income, and since I was making lots of money Bill and I decided to build a house in Wellfleet. It was during that time that we decided to get tested.

    In hindsight it's clear to me that Bill was getting sick, fevers, night sweats. Luckily we had a whole language to talk about feelings, one we had learned in sobriety. A lot of the basic grammar of Alcoholics Anonymous is learning to live consciously, to examine what's going on in your life. Even so, it was a confusing, tumultuous time. Many of our friends had already died. We were beginning a life of loss.

I'm not sure that people outside this [Provincetown] community can imagine what it's like to lose thirty friends. I'm very close to my [biological] family, but even as I try to share this experience with them I realize that no one in my family has thirty close friends. That extended circle of friends is special to gay culture, I think. Since we're accustomed to being an abused minority, we bond with one another for protection and comfort—we form extended families. So when you lose "friends" to AIDS, most of them are really "family."

Anyway, Bill and I figured we'd both be negative or we'd both be positive. As it turned out, he tested positive and I tested "inconclusive." I went the next day for retesting, waiting for two weeks for the result: negative. I have subsequently remained negative whenever I've been tested.

Pam: How did Bill deal with you being negative?

It was very difficult for him. I don't know if he ever dealt with it, or whether he just vented his anger about his own diagnosis.

The whole question of how positives and negatives interact with one another is very complicated. Being negative, especially for a man my age—late thirties, forties—is a significant part of one's identity. As a sexual issue, clearly, positive men are afraid of rejection and negative men are afraid of infection. But it goes far beyond sexual relations—it permeates people's attitudes, the way they think about themselves and their futures.

Being HIV-negative is a real qualifier of who I am and how I am perceived by my closest community: gay men. My sisters, for example don't think of themselves as HIV-negatives. My lesbian friends don't, for the most part, identify themselves that way. But I can't avoid thinking about it all the time.

I went to a weekend workshop at the Support Group a couple of years ago. It was called "HIV+ and HIV- Gay Men: Mending the Splits." All of us who went—mostly HIV+ guys because they outnumber the negatives here—but all of us said initially, "What splits, what splits?" But all around us on the walls of the meeting room were posters, maybe twenty of them; each one had an example of the splits between positive and negative gay men. They were dead-on accurate, terrifyingly so. We were surrounded by proofs of the splits.

We need to address this much more carefully. We need to find ways to bridge some of the gaps. I've heard a lot of people say that AIDS has taught the gay community how to care for itself and how to love one another in a different way. I don't agree with that. I think that a wider sense of loving is an intrinsic part of being gay. The AIDS epidemic, how the community has responded, has simply given the larger culture a vivid picture of this, one expressed in socially acceptable terms.

Pam: I have found that almost everyone says that AIDS has changed the way people—in this case we'll say men—value life. Could that not include loving as well as living?

Oh yes, yes. I wholeheartedly agree that AIDS has developed people's capacities to love and to value life. *Developed*, not created. That's an important distinction. I don't think disease can create, but rather it refines what was already there—intensifies it. Who knows what we might have learned as gay people if AIDS hadn't come along? For example, prior to AIDS in intensely gay communities like San Francisco there was a whole movement forming—one pointed toward gay families. Gay men and lesbians were having babies together, inventing alternative family structures. It made perfect sense; it still makes perfect sense. AIDS stopped short, in its tracks, in an instant, the whole possibility of gay men having children. How might that possibility have affected the development of how gay men love?

Pam: It would have changed the way people think about families, about what constitutes a family.

I guess the point I'm making is that life without AIDS wouldn't have been identical to life before AIDS. We've lost fifteen years. I'll be forty this April and I've been dealing with AIDS since I was twenty-six.

Pam: I want to get back to Bill again. Can you finish that history?

Bill was diagnosed positive at Thanksgiving. The following June we finished building the house—Bill's brother built it and the three of us designed it—and Bill was diagnosed with AIDS the week we moved in. He lived ten months.

Pam: Were you the sole caretaker?

Oh no, not at all. His mother who lived half a mile from us, his brother who had lived next door until we built the house, his sister, Shirley who lived in Maine, all helped me care for Bill. The last few weeks before he died his sister and mother lived in our house. Actually Gladys, Bill's mother, and his brother returned to help me with David, my second lover. Right before he died, they just kind of "knew" and showed up. There's a larger community of support too. When David died and I had to put his memorial service together, most of the guys who helped were guys as sick as he had been, people who knew him from support groups, from riding in the van together to Boston. I can't imagine what it must feel like to be dealing with opportunistic infections yourself and do a program, do flowers for someone else, do a memorial for someone else.

Pam: So you've lost two lovers to AIDS?

Yes, and the guy I'm seeing now is HIV+. We've talked a lot about that. He asked me, as everybody asks me, "How can you get involved with somebody who is positive?"

I told Peter, "Why would you want to date me: look at my record, I've buried two lovers!" After we got done laughing we began to explore what it means to live in the present, or what is sacrificed when you refuse to live in the "now."

For me one of the most difficult parts of AIDS is all the waiting. Waiting to get sick, waiting to get better, waiting for test
results, waiting for new medications. Waiting, waiting, waiting,
waiting. I need to take the "now" and live it the best way I can.

Peter Warnock

Peter Warnock's engaging smile, easy repartee, and talent for impromptu
entertainment equipped him well to preside over the Atlantic House
Bar for sixteen years. The fabled "A-House" is steeped in Provincetown
cultural history. Thoreau mentions it as the Inn where he intends to
lodge; it resonates with the echoes of Billie Holiday, Nina Simone,
and Eartha Kitt who sang in its smoky recesses in the early days of
their legendary careers. Peter Warnock has heard more than most in
his thirty-eight years. He shies away from few subjects, including his
own ten-year HIV diagnosis, the alterations that diagnosis has brought,
his burgeoning relationship with John Culver. The transformations in
his own life still seem to surprise him, and he handles his new discov-
eries gently, like something crystal that still has the potential to shat-
ter.

    I was born on the North Shore of Boston and grew up in
Marblehead. My first trip to Provincetown occurred after I
graduated from high school, and I moved down here in 1978,
Memorial Day weekend. The first three years I was seasonal.
During the early '80s the year-round population began to swell,
and with lots more people, more things to do, I began to stay
here all year. Originally I worked at a guest house and at night
as a cocktail waiter at the Atlantic House. When the A-House
got a year-round license I got a job bartending there. I had a
steady income. Off-season it's minimal, but during the summer it was very lucrative—a couple hundred bucks a night.
All summer long.

I worked my way up from cocktail waiter through bartender to the manager—doing all the liquor ordering, all the supplies, all the scheduling, all the hiring and firing. And I was HIV+. I knew from 1986 on about my diagnosis.

Gradually I realized that I just had to quit at the A-House, had to quit being in that atmosphere, the noise, the drugs, the drinking. It was all take, take, take—and take on my part too, just pulling in the bucks. I quit in February of '95.

Probably around April, Jennifer Justice officiated at a memorial service for a friend of mine. I was just overwhelmed by her presence. Even though I was still drinking, I started to go to the UU church. And slowly I had this transformation. I've always loved to sing and I decided I wanted to join the choir, get in there and lend my voice. That turned out to be a spiritual journey I hadn't anticipated, I hadn't known I was even looking for. It fulfilled something in me.

Having been a bartender in a very popular club, I know many facets of the town and the people in it. But I wanted to move outside the party atmosphere. So I did some volunteering at PASG, joined the UU choir, decided to clean up my act.

Pam: What did you do at PASG?

In the past I delivered lunches to eighteen or twenty people. By the time I stopped delivering meals, nine of the twenty were gone. Primarily what I did was drive the van to Boston. I knew Boston well from growing up there and I really enjoyed providing that service, delivering people to their doctors' appointments. Now—[long pause] now I get the meals I used to deliver, and I ride in the van I used to drive. I have guilt feelings about that; I feel I should still be able to get out there and help once a week. But I have a lot of neuropathy in my legs and I just can't handle it anymore.

Pam: You mentioned cleaning up your act; are you in recovery?

Yeah, pretty much. I'm not a hundred percent successful, but I consider it a success story for me. I met John through the UU church and of course he's in complete recovery, fourteen years on April 1st. So I chose April 1st as the day I'd cut alcohol and cigarettes completely. But that turned out to be the day I was diagnosed with Kaposi's Sarcoma.

Pam: So now you have an AIDS diagnosis?

In Massachusetts, below a 200 T-cell count is [defined as] full-blown AIDS. Then you qualify for all the programs like drug reimbursement, disability, Medicare, and Mass. Health. But I've always considered an opportunistic infection to mean full-blown AIDS. I have friends who have died of PCP [Pneumo-cystis Pneumonia] who would look normal one week and were dead the next.

When I first came to Provincetown HIV was not known. It was just one big community of all ages, no cliques, no special interest groups—like the body-beautiful gym crowd. I made a lot of good, close friends who I thought I'd know forever, folks who would be my friends into my 60s and 70s. When HIV began to cut people down—you start to question the wisdom of getting close to people. After a while you ask, how close do you want to get to a person who will be dead in two or three years? I've lost thirty or forty friends, people I had Christmas dinners with, spent Thanksgiving with, people whose families I got to know. It's devastating. And now, at thirty-eight, I'm looking at my own "twilight years." I think that's what prompts me to do volunteer work. Maybe I'll never be remembered, but at least I'm helping while I'm here and leaving a little bit of a mark.

Pam: What kind of volunteer work are you doing now?

Right now I'm on a working committee of the AIDS ministry. We're starting a memorial registration where you go in, talk to Jennifer or Ed—or whoever the new AIDS minister is going to be. Be interviewed. Let them find out a bit about you, who you are, before you die. And what kind of service—readings, music—you want. Whether you want cremation. How it's going to be paid for.

Too often in the past when somebody dies and his family has disowned him, five or six friends have had to band together to try to organize a service, in most cases to pay for it out of pocket.

The memorial registry used me as a template, interviewing me as a test case for this process. I also was the team captain for the AIDS Walk for the UU church.

Pam: Does the physical environment provide you with any spiritual nourishment?

There is enormous beauty here. And even though it sounds like a cliché, there is also a groundedness here, something you really miss when you go away. The minute you come over that hill in North Truro something happens in your heart. It jumps up into your throat. I still gasp after eighteen years.

Pam: And clearly your new relationship with John is a welcome one?

Oh-h-h, the kicker. John is HIV negative. We pussyfooted around seeing each other for some time.

Pam: And are you surprised at yourself?

I'm more surprised at John, someone who's had two lovers die of AIDS in fourteen years, now hooking up with someone who's HIV+. We were just talking today about the future, since he's filling out his application for the Peace Corps. It takes a year for them to process the application and accept him. But that works, since he has another year for his associate's degree in nursing.

I said today "Why don't you just move to Provincetown and we'll get a nice place on the beach. Or join VISTA and stay home." But you know I would love him less if he didn't follow his heart, do what he wants to do. He's got dreams.

And plans. And goals. I do too, but I don't kid myself. Perhaps I live vicariously through him.

My goals are less long-range, more yearly. I want to live to see forty. I'd like to see the new millennium come in. I have these stepping stones I want to achieve.

John has been a great stabilizer in my life, making me realize that I too have something to offer—whether it's lending my voice to the choir, or driving somebody to the doctor for an appointment, or team-captaining a walk that probably raised $1,500 for AIDS.

I try to give in the ways I can, even when it's pretty painful. Singing in the John Thomas "Beloved Companions" composition at this year's vigil was very, very difficult for me. I had lost two very close friends this year, and when I read the words for the piece I just broke down. But I did it, and later I got a personal note from John Thomas thanking me for participating. In how many communities would that happen?

Pam: How's your health?

Real good, right now. It's kind of like a headache in the back of your head; if it's there long enough, that's what normal feels like. Granted, there are days when my neuropathy [painful nerve damage in the extremities] makes me not even want to walk downtown to get the mail—but I have a pretty high threshold for pain. I'm in it for the long haul and I'm going to do the best I can.

Pam: Are you trying any of these new protease inhibitors?

No. The way the protease inhibitors were explained to me by my doctor was that, if you're on a sinking ship and you have one flare left, if you shoot it off there's no way to bring it back. So unless you're really at the point where you need the protease inhibitors, it's not desirable to get on them. But I know people who are on them and I know how promising they are. So I have that to look forward to.

Before I needed a primary care physician in Boston, Lenny Alberts was my doctor right here in Provincetown, and I have all the respect in the world for him. He goes to all the AIDS conferences, stays right at the forefront of new treatments. I cannot comprehend what he's seen and gone through in his years here—they must be so incredible. So we have a lot going for us here.

I remember once flying back to the States from Germany, and as the plane was hitting the East Coast it went right over Cape Cod. I literally ran over to the other side of the plane to see "home." Eight or ten other people crowded around me as I explained the configuration. "See that little spit of land? That is Cape Cod and right at its tip is Provincetown." There's something special here: the light, the color, air, the people. The *people*. Even at 30,000 feet this community looks good.

Dennis Miles

Dennis Miles shares Peter Warnock's desire to live to see the millennium. In his case, living to see the turn of the century will ensure that as he puts it, "my grandchildren will be old enough to remember me." He shares with John Culver the experience of losing a lover to AIDS, and he struggles as both Peter and John do with ways of being of service to the AIDS community. A soft-spoken private man, Dennis identifies the loss of independence as being his greatest fear. Although he understands that his compromised immune system forces him into a series of precautions, he doesn't want his life to be steered by AIDS. He speaks in the short declarative sentences of a realist.

Pam: [Pointing to photographs on the coffee table.] Are these your children?

Yes. My two babies and their two babies. My son Scott will be twenty-four this year, and Janet, my daughter, will be twenty-one. They live in Plymouth. They know about my diagnosis and are supportive.

I've only been in Provincetown three years, although I was born on the Cape. My father was in the Army and I grew up as an Army brat. We lived in Missouri, Illinois, Taiwan. I have an older sister, an older brother, and a twin brother, identical twin. My sister lives with my parents, helps to take care of them. Both my brothers live in Michigan. My sister is my best friend and support. We've always been extremely close, but AIDS cemented that. My twin is having a difficult time dealing with my diagnosis. He had a hard time when he found out I was gay, but we've bridged that gap. I know we'll bridge the HIV gap too. Identical twins have a special bond; disruption is very painful. My older brother—well, he doesn't know and won't know. He's very disturbed, under the care of a therapist.

I married right out of high school; my ex-wife's name is Laura, and we were married for thirteen years. I knew I was different, but not that I was gay. I thought that family life with Laura would stabilize everything; that little fairy tale fell apart real quick. [Laughter.]

We separated, got divorced, and I gradually came out of the closet. I met Lee at work; we were both in retail management. We were together four years, and after he got sick he only survived seven months. They determined he had full-blown AIDS at the time of testing.

Pam: What was it like for you?

A nightmare. A horrifying nightmare. At first I just couldn't believe it. It came out of the blue. He was only twenty-nine. They also suggested immediately that I be tested, saying that since Lee had had AIDS the entire time we were together it was very likely that I'd be positive too.

Pam: So at the time you were struggling with his illness, his dying, you were also dealing with the knowledge of your own HIV status.

Ironically, I wasn't. I never thought of my condition. He was just so sick, needed so much care, that all the attention diverted to him. Basically it was a twenty-four-hour-a-day ordeal. It never really occurred to me that I was infected until months after his death.

I think during his illness I just went into overdrive. He had respiratory distress, heart problems, he went blind, had a brain infection. He suffered a great deal of pain, was on morphine. To watch a twenty-nine-year-old healthy man of about 145 pounds turn into a sixty-pound skeleton in seven months is not an easy thing. Right then I determined I couldn't have a relationship with anybody who is negative.

Pam: When you addressed your own diagnosis after Lee died, how did you deal with it?

It took a while. And it was easy to deny because I was basically healthy. I had a very simple picture of HIV after Lee. Once Lee got sick he never got any better. That was my picture: "You get sick, you die." I started to do some reading, some research and realized that I had to talk with others. I went to see Janice Walk, and through her help and that of the support group I've learned more about the disease and how to live with it. I accepted that I was HIV+. As a matter of fact, I have an AIDS diagnosis now. That changes the way you think. Material things aren't important anymore; career isn't important anymore. What is important to me are my children, my family. I came from a close-knit family. I'm fortunate to have parents who are elderly but still healthy. And last year I was surprised by the birth of my two grandchildren. That opens up a whole new chapter. It's something I never expected to see and I'm having a whole lot of joy with the grandchildren.

Pam: Do you use the services of PASG?

Oh yes, oh yes. The support there is irreplaceable. Dealing with medical problems and disability is horrendous in this country, absolutely horrendous. How wonderful to call your case manager and say, "I'm overwhelmed," and he says "Drop everything and bring it over here." That kind of help is a Godsend. And their patience breeds patience. They've been through all the steps, know how long it takes, how and when it will happen. That gets me calm and focused.

The support groups have also been vital, as has the larger Provincetown community. With the groups and throughout the community I still have my own identity. I'm not looked on as a person with AIDS, or as a person who used to be in retail management. I'm still Dennis, a father, a grandfather, a person who has a purpose in life, who can set goals.

I'm so independent, I so fear losing my independence that I suppose I'll need to work on that: on what happens when I can't cook for myself, or vacuum my own house, or what happens when I have to give up the car. The support group teaches you to focus on what's happening now and face what lies ahead when it comes and not before.

But that's a struggle. For example, I learned recently that all the immunizations I had as a child are useless now. They've all broken down. When the immune system breaks down you're open to whooping cough, measles, mumps, chicken pox, polio, anything. So do I play with my grandchildren or not? Is it worth going to church or not? It takes some thinking to convince yourself not to live like a hermit.

Pam: What are your goals right now?

I want to stay healthy enough to live to the year 2002 for three reasons. One, I'll see the turn of the century; two, I'll live to see the age of fifty; three, most important, my grandchildren will each be seven and they'll be old enough to remember me. Hopefully, with God's grace and the miracles of science, I may still be alive at that time. Then I'll set a new goal.

ॐ

Mark Doty

Mark Doty is much taller, more substantial than the photos on the dust jackets of his books suggest. He generously agreed to wedge an interview between digging out from the January blizzard and catching a flight to London where he was nominated for (and subsequently awarded) the T.S. Eliot Prize for Poetry.

Since much of his poetry focuses on his life as a gay man and on his eleven-and-a-half-year relationship with Wally Roberts, who died of AIDS in January of 1994, I knew he'd have no difficulty addressing my questions. What I hadn't anticipated was the way his story would unfold—one seamless chronological and associative whole, unrolling like a word-drenched scroll. Perhaps this was the consequence of writing about the same events in *Heaven's Coast* (a memoir published in 1996), he volunteered. Or perhaps it was simply a narrative acid-etched in memory.

Mark has the well-modulated voice of the teacher and public reader that he is. When searching for exactly the right word he pauses, tongue on the tip of his teeth, makes a selection and moves on. He wears fashionable round wire-rims, eyeglasses I heard someone (who was introducing him at a later poetry reading) compare to those of a Russian revolutionary like Trotsky. Anton Chekhov seems a better comparison—the writer who caught the crisis of a culture in achingly muted, complexly nuanced language.

We began by talking about his decision to turn to memoir (*Heaven's Coast*, the story of the last years of Wally Roberts' life, was "in press" in January of '96) after having published three very successful volumes of poetry.

Jeanne: Did you turn to narrative because it allowed greater freedom?

Yes, I think so. I felt so much and what I felt was so overwhelming that, in a way, there was too much pressure to create a poem ... too much emotional weight on every word, every line. And the reasons were practical too. A while back a friend had asked me to contribute something to a prose book. At that time Wally had lost use of his legs, was in a wheelchair, but was still pretty alert. I wrote a short piece about those days and set it aside. Then just before he died I got an invitation to write an essay for a book on gay men and religion. That's provocative for me now, I thought, but there's no way I can write it now. Maybe six weeks after Wally died I was washing the dishes and I thought, for some reason, of that project. If I were going to write that essay, if I were able to write that essay, this is what I'd say. So I went to the computer and wrote a sentence, then another sentence. Really it was like putting one foot in front of the other in the dark. I didn't know for a while if it would ever be a book, but I knew that it was something I needed to make, especially in that year when I felt as if I were stumbling around in the wreckage of my life.

So I just followed the thread, and about four essays or so into the project, I showed it to an editor who was interested in publishing my poetry. He was very enthusiastic, believed in it as a whole, so suddenly I felt as if I was given permission to continue this work that I really didn't know how to do.

Jeanne: Does it deal with the years after Wally was diagnosed, or does it range over wider experience?

The present tense of the book is the first year after his death, that period of intense grief, of trying to survive the sense of being blindsided. Then it flashes back to moments in the history of our relationship and the period of his illness.

Jeanne: You were in Vermont prior to coming here?

We lived in Vermont for five years—from 1985 to 1990.

Jeanne: What precipitated the move to Provincetown?

There were lots of factors. We had gone to Vermont because I had gotten a teaching job at Goddard College. I had been teaching part time in Boston, so the idea of a full-time job was exciting: Goddard was also an interesting place to go—it was one of the few schools in the country, at that time anyway, that offered tuition rebates and other benefits for same-sex couples. It had no pre-established curriculum, but instead the faculty would sit down at the beginning of each semester and decide the course of study. Very progressive, endlessly entertaining, a constantly chaotic place.

So the job was attractive, and going to Vermont, out of Boston's real estate market, meant that we could buy a house, make a home together, make a history in the way couples like to do. I had a grant from the Massachusetts Arts Foundation; it was not that much money, but it was a fortune for us, enough to make a down payment on an incredibly ramshackle Victorian house in Montpelier. It had a flat roof, it was a huge Victorian thing, and just about everything needed work: insulation, new roof, new furnace, new plumbing.

The first winter we lived there I remember I couldn't type because the house was so cold my fingers got stiff. We had one dramatic adventure after another there. The positive side was that we could have a home, garden, dogs, cats. But it was also an isolating place to live. Our friends were all from the college, and they were either straight couples or lesbians. We didn't know any other gay male couples. A town of 8,000 people and we were it. We also lived in a working-class, old-Vermonter neighborhood. We were the guys from Massachusetts who were fixing up the house. I remember one elderly neighbor who used to stand on the sidewalk watching us fixing up the house. One day he called out, "Where are your women?" [Laughter.]

So it was fine to be there together, to make a home together, but once Wally tested positive it didn't seem so fine anymore. The preeminent fact of our reality was HIV, yet it was not visible in our community. It was as if we had this crisis, yet everything else continued on in exactly the same way. That made for a crazy dissonance between the way we were experiencing the world and the way our community was experiencing the world.

At that time in Vermont there were about 20 people with AIDS. There was a fledgling little support service in Burlington, forty-five minutes away. So it was very difficult.

Additionally, Wally had a small business as a window display designer and, since he had never been to college, he was going to Goddard, working towards a B.A. Both of these things, in light of his diagnosis, suddenly seemed questionable. His business wasn't that satisfying, and school felt oriented toward the future when the future was compromised, in question. It was as if we were delaying gratification, working for the future, and suddenly that seemed silly.

That winter two friends of ours were spending their sabbatical in Provincetown. They invited us to visit and I've never felt so welcomed. A big storm blew up that weekend so, of course, we had to stay. [Laughter.] And when we went back to Vermont it occurred to us that we could come back for Spring Break. That week showed us what it felt like not to have to wear the kind of armor we wore in Vermont. We could be gay people, people living with HIV, and we didn't have to put energy into protecting ourselves. The less fear and tension you hold, the more you are able to respond freely and openly to life.

So we began to think very seriously about moving. And suddenly everything moved into place allowing us to come to Provincetown. First I was offered a teaching job at Sarah

Lawrence, outside of New York, one that only required me to be there a couple of consecutive days a week. Some friends offered to buy our house and suddenly here we were, living in a little winter rental on the beach, a spot we stayed in for nine months. It was glorious. It was 1990, and remember, that was the year that the summer just seemed to go on and on—finally melding into a long golden autumn. I remember so vividly sitting at my desk watching Wally and the dog on the beach, playing, swimming for hours and hours. I remember them going out into that long, long expanse of silver and gold that the bay becomes at low tide. We were very, very happy.

During that fall we started looking for houses, found the house on Pearl Street and set about getting it in shape. During that winter when we were working on it I think I noticed the first real shift in his health. It's hard now to know if it was depression, or if it was the very beginning of the condition that would ultimately take his life.

He died of something called PML, Progressive multifocal leucoencephalopathy, a viral brain infection. It's one of those viruses that most of us have, harmless until your immune system is compromised. He began to have these bouts of depression; then it crystallized quite vividly one day. I was in New York, Wally was walking Arden, not on a leash, one winter day—out to the Breakwater. Arden saw a rabbit and took off across Commercial Street. Wally heard brakes squealing and a terrible thump as Arden was hit by a car. The dog yelped and took off running. Wally couldn't locate him, didn't know how hurt he was, how disoriented. He called me, I came home and searched too; eventually a friend found Arden the next day walking along the street in a daze. He brought him home. That experience, Arden's vulnerability, seemed to be for Wally a kind of metaphor for his own vulnerability. A great despair came over him. He would work hard against it, but it was very, very, difficult. He did start seeing a wonderful therapist in town whose clientele was almost exclusively people with HIV.

That proved to be a very good experience and went on until his death.

Jeanne: Were there other support services that either Wally or you availed yourselves of? Were you involved in PASG at all?

Well, at that time he was positive but asymptomatic. He had more than 200 T-cells, so he could not be classified as having AIDS. We both eventually began to go to support groups in town. Even after his AIDS diagnosis it was problematic for Wally because he never got any of the "classic" opportunistic infections which are markers of that diagnosis.

As time went on through '91 and '92 he gradually lost his energy, he was troubled by headaches, he had a general sense of malaise. Eventually he was clearly incapacitated, could barely get off the couch, but he still didn't officially have AIDS. His doctor said, "you can have the diagnosis now if you want," which is, of course, in some practical ways beneficial. It means a lot of help in terms of services and benefits. People in Provincetown really know how to negotiate the maze of SSI, of SSDI, of food stamps, Medicaid, all those entitlements that a person working alone can't possibly decipher.

You can say, "Well, I'm already sick and to say I have AIDS is just to add a word to it." But what a *word*. Eventually our struggle became a moot point because CDC changed the definition of AIDS to include people with less than 200 T-cells just as Wally's count fell below that. Suddenly he had AIDS and those services became available.

When he did get an AIDS diagnosis, this complex machine went into gear. He was eligible for help through the Family Care Program, which meant that I could be paid a small stipend to take care of him so that he wouldn't need nursing care. That little extra income helped with the expenses that were crippling us. That program also meant that he had regular visits from a social worker who helped us think about the problems we were facing, particularly the long process of accommodating to his limits. I could go to a support group for caregivers that the social workers from the Family Care Program facilitated. That was helpful in a jolting way. It was a group that shifted population fairly frequently as people died and as new caregivers appeared. The people for whom we were caring were often at very different stages of the illness. Wally was still functioning pretty well when I started, so that was my context, and then I'd go to a meeting where someone had gone blind that week, or had a tracheotomy, or had discovered lymphoma. There was that continual confrontation with reality that was both necessary and awful at the same time. That's the human paradox. We set up all kinds of things to cushion ourselves from it, but we crave reality. It's the thing we most need, are most consoled by—the acknowledgment of what is real. I think my two-year participation in that group was helpful for Wally too. He was confronting his own mortality and he didn't need to confront my pain and anger and terror about the whole thing.

This gradual process of Wally's weakening continued, usually not a dramatic change but rather as a continuous erosion. I'll never forget one day when I was out walking on the dunes and I looked across the moors and saw a man with a black dog walking down the hillside. I thought, "Oh, great! It's Wally and Arden coming out to meet me." And then I realized Wally can't walk like that. And then I realized this is not going to happen ever anymore. It's that kind of moment that draws a line of demarcation. That measures the descent.

By the summer of '92 Wally had pretty much taken to the couch. After Christmas in early '93 we went to Florida together. I was invited to teach a writing workshop and we thought it would be nice for Wally to come along. Even if he was sitting on the couch it would be a different couch in a different place and the weather would be warm. It was extremely difficult for him to manage. We would take little trips in our rented car, go sit by the beach and eat a sandwich, but I could really see that things were going badly. I remember him saying with an awful kind of resignation in his voice, "This will be my last trip."

In March I was teaching in New York when the town nurse, who checked on him periodically, called me to say Wally had fallen and had been unable to get up. He had gone very quickly from feeling a little uncertain on his legs, particularly on steps, to just losing the use of his legs.

I came home immediately and that was the point when I saw the system of care for people with AIDS in Provincetown really begin to function. It was remarkable. In the space of a few days we had a nurse from the VNA, we could have home health aides who could help with a variety of things, we could have a physical therapist come to work with him; his therapist began to come to the house. A wave of people.

In some ways it was a mixed blessing. We had been the sort of couple that is pretty self-sufficient; we enjoyed a sense of intimacy and privacy in our home. Suddenly there was this army of people. I found myself looking around from time to time grumbling to myself, "Who are you and where are my forks?"

But what I gradually realized was that I could relinquish some of my caretaking duties into the hands of these good, responsible people. It was good for me and good for Wally because he could have some relationships with other people, a possibility that had been foreclosed when he was confined.

In the summer of '93 Wally's mental life began to shift. Again it was very subtle, so it's hard for me to decipher exactly when it happened. But gradually I became aware that instead of him saying what he felt or thought, that I was interpreting what he felt, what he thought. By the end of the summer of '93 I had to go back to work and was really troubled by the thought of being away from home three days a week. Wally had formed a very sweet relationship with one of the home health aides, Darren. As it turned out, Darren was looking for an apartment, so I asked him if he would be interested in living on the second floor of our house in exchange for taking care of Wally on the days I was at school. It was wonderful for Wally to have a friend there, one who had the ability to turn the indignities of illness into little jokes; and it was wonderful for me to have another healthy person in the house, to be a reality check on me when I would lose my perspective.

By the fall of '93 Wally had really begun to fail. In November I had a birthday party for him, a surprise, and I invited his family to come. Although he couldn't take too much at one time, we really had a nice time. His parents came in the morning, friends came in the afternoon, but I don't think it was until that evening that it registered that this was a surprise. For him.

The birthday party was so much fun that we decided to have a Christmas party—just two weeks later. But in the space of two weeks control of language started to slip. One side of his mouth started to turn down. He was like someone who'd had a stroke. He would reach for a word, find the wrong word, recognize he had said something strange and then laugh about it. This is also about the time we got Beau, the golden retriever pup I found at the shelter, and who proved irresistible. So here's this crazed Golden Retriever running around; I think Wally's therapist decided I had really lost my mind.

When school ended for me it was pretty clear that Wally just wanted to be with me. Darren went home for the holidays and so we had Christmas by ourselves. The snow piled up outside and inside the house we had this little island of intimacy.

I played music, cooked meals and fed him, sat by his bed and read. Sometimes we talked a little until the effort of finding words tired him. For some reason I decided I had to write and I tried to work in my study next door even though every five minutes or so Wally called out, "Babe, I need something to eat," or "I need the remote." Usually interruptions like these would finish me, but this time the process was completely different. It snowed and snowed and we grew closer and closer.

In January just as I was beginning to think that there was no way I'd be able to return to school, I received an Ingram Merrill Foundation grant, enabling me to be at home with Wally. The time was short and very deep. A few friends came to say good-bye. By now his eyes were closed, although when he opened his right eye just a tiny bit, I could tell he could see —- just that angle of vision. So one day, very close to the end, I got the two cats, Thisbe and Portia, and Arden and Beau, and I lined them all up on the bed in the line of vision. We stayed for a while in his corridor of sight.

Have you ever experienced someone dying? The heat and the light of it? The shine around it? I could feel a quality of energy around him. And I swear I had a clear image of Wally leaping free, leaping out of his body. He had been so ready to go. It was as if some space opened in the wall behind his head and he leapt out through that space. The room had a kind of humming intensity, a resonance. I could feel the whole space vibrating. You know, that tuning-fork kind of reverberation? I could feel his liberation and also his presence, as if seeing from both sides of the veil.

In a passage from *Heaven's Coast*, Mark Doty captures life's uniqueness and tenuousness by describing the sea lavender so abundant at Hatches Harbor, the place where he scattered Wally's ashes.

"We are elements of the world's consciousness of itself, and thus we are necessary: replaceable and irreplaceable at once. Someone will take our places, but then again there will never be anyone like us, no one who will see quite this way; we are a sudden flowering of seeing, among millions of such blossomings. Like the innumerable tiny stars on the branching stalk of the sea lavender; it takes how many, a thousand, to construct this violet sheen, this little shaking cloud of flowers."

Chapter Six

Race Point

In her book chronicling months of living in Henry Beston's tiny cottage on Cape Cod's Outer Beach, *Journey to the Outermost House*, Nan Waldron describes a shrine in Japan which serves as an analogue for her feelings about the beach. Shinto Spirit Home of Yoshida purportedly shines with an intense white light, she reports. "There is no altar, no icons, no images of worship—just a space in which to feel the light."

Race Point is such a space, where sand and sea fuse in a seamless bowl of light. This is the "lookout spot" where past and present, discovery and self-discovery, shoulder into one another. There is a sense of natural drama at Race Point, something old and elemental which confers both context and scale on the human dramas that have occurred close to its shore. The scene of very specific dangers at the beginning of the century, Race Point offers a vantage point from which to see other dangers threatening those who navigate the closing years of this century.

From the observation post atop Race Point National Seashore Visitor Center, three points stand out on the horizon, monuments to another time, to a set of perils different from those that haunt the final years of this century. Race Point Lighthouse is the tallest; then, to the right, the Coast Guard Station, and farther to the right still, the weathered shingle outline of the Old Harbor Life Saving Station—moved to this spot from Chatham when beach erosion threatened it in 1977.

In the years that bracketed the turn of the century, before the Cape Cod Canal was built, ships were required to sail around the Outer Cape, negotiating all the dangerous shoals and sudden sprung rip tides along the peninsula. In 1872 nine life-saving stations were built and manned by the U.S. Life Saving Service, two of them in Provincetown, at Race Point and Peaked Hill Bars. In 1896 four other stations were added, among them Wood End in Provincetown. For more than forty years, men assigned to these stations patrolled the beaches for signs of ships in distress or for signs of shipwrecked survivors.

Each station was assigned a "keeper"—a year-round position of high authority—as well as a team of "surfmen" who worked from August 1st through the winter and spring to June 1st. Crews were responsible not only for their own maintenance and that of their equipment, but also they were expected to practice rescue drills with regularity. The drills included the launching of twenty-four-foot surfboats, the deployment of smaller Coast Guard dories, and mastery of the Lyle gun-breeches buoy apparatus, a system of ropes and pulleys designed to rescue men on ships in distress when seas were too violent to launch a boat. The Lyle gun shot out a rescue line from shore; once affixed to the boat, breeches buoys—canvas seats resembling breeches with a buoyant waistband—were attached so that shipwrecked survivors could be hauled in over the line to safety. Surfmen had to be physically fit, excellent swimmers and boatmen; they also had to possess a genuine measure of courage to attempt rescues in winter waters.

George Bryant, Provincetown historian who had several relatives in the life-saving service, is wary of romanticizing surfmen, of assuming too easily that they were "angels of mercy." In fact their motives were practical, he suggests. Since wages for serving at a station were quite high by the standards of the time and surfmen could supplement their income by fishing in the summer months, the job was fairly lucrative. The life-saving service was born out of necessity, not altruism, and supported by men seeking a good livelihood.

Bryant suggests that the real tragedy of the all-too-frequent ship-wrecks at the turn of the century lay with the privation of survivors left behind. When husbands were lost, their widows and children "could expect to be ruined for at least one, perhaps two generations," he writes. "The *Cora S. McKay* was one such example, a fishing schooner lost on the Grand Banks in September, 1900. Thirty men died; 54 children were left fatherless. Although Provincetown supplied funds for some months and the churches helped out as they could, without a system like social security there was no continuing support to depend on." The lesson of the life saving stations is not simply who could be rescued, but who could not. Many more lives were lost than those drowned at sea.

Although AIDS remains proportionally a "gay male disease" in Prov-incetown, those "other lost lives" that Bryant evokes when speaking of sea tragedies have their counterpoint in the as-yet largely "invisible" female HIV+ population in the community. The problems women face with HIV are difficult everywhere: since the disease manifests in different ways for women, often their diagnosis is delayed, their symp-toms misread. Frequently they serve as their children's sole support, so that the decisions they make directly affect lives beyond their own. And additionally, in a community like Provincetown where caregiving models have been designed to assist gay males, women's needs have not been adequately addressed.

In the late summer of 1996 Carole and Wendy volunteered to contribute their stories to this collection. Irene Cramer, a Provincetown therapist who runs a support group specifically for women who are HIV+, provides a frame for their stories by discussing some common concerns women with AIDS share and what she believes is necessary in order to break the isolation many feel in the community.

Irene Cramer

Irene Cramer has, by her own estimate, "been coming to Provincetown since I was a child." Her wide range of experience as a therapist, a researcher, and an administrator equips her with the authority of an eyewitness, an invited guest at the table of many of the crucial debates in current managed health care. Soft-spoken, unassuming, an opponent might mistake her equipoise for pliancy. That would be an error of monumental proportions, since beneath the calm exterior she percolates with pressing concerns: the latest statistics on breast cancer, outrage at the monopolies of some pharmaceutical companies, the plight of the urban poor, the as-yet insufficiently defined distinctions between what living with HIV means for men as opposed to what it means for women.

As the child of Holocaust survivors, Irene finds herself particularly drawn to men and women who live in the long shadow of premature death. She has a special reverence for oral history, for the ways in which people's stories name the nameless, preserve a culture, generate a way to think about the future. She calls herself, with unconscious eloquence, "simply a listener. The stories are what I hear and what I respond to."

Jeanne: Am I right that when you moved to Provincetown a year ago you took over Katina Rodis's group at PASG, the men's group that was featured in the *Shooting Stars* film?

> That's right. When Katina had surgery I moved into that amazing group of men for a time. Of course they all knew one another so well that I just moved very slowly, finding my way. Some helped me enormously, like Victor, who shared some of the same cultural background I come from. His death this August was very painful.
>
> Later when I recognized the need for a women's group, I started that up. The women's group meets weekly now.

Jeanne: What were you doing prior to coming to Provincetown?

I worked in the Worcester area for many years; I was an administrator and I had a private practice. I went back to get my Ph.D at Brandeis, got up to the dissertation stage. But when my partner Judith was diagnosed with breast cancer, I had to redesign my schedule to be flexible when I was needed.

In Worcester I worked with people who had been long-time residents of that post-industrial city and who were dealing with the whole range of issues associated with those hardships; raising children, working at the same job year after year, what happens with the aging process. I also worked with people with serious medical or emotional problems and with the AIDS Project in Worcester, where I was on the board in the '80s. I think I learned about the experiences of the native community—and those experiences really aren't very different from the native community in Provincetown. What you see are life problems: substance abuse, domestic violence, aging. In Provincetown, however, the community is so small and so isolated that it all gets entwined.

Of course in addition to the native community, there is a whole other group of people who have deliberately chosen to come to Provincetown. Some have come to heal themselves. Some have decided to make a life turn: "I've been living this way, now I want to do it differently." Some come out of a need to be connected to others in a small community, and find ways—whether through AA, or a church, or theater, or the community chorus—to make that vital connection.

I think I began to realize with new force the importance of people's stories at the end of Judith's life. Whether people are young or old, dying prematurely or in their time, hearing their voices is so essential. Judith was an energetic, smart, assertive, creative, and impatient person who could not find her own voice to talk about the cancer she died with. She could talk about virtually anything else—so her death took me to a place that reaffirmed what I have always wanted to do: work that ensures that people find a way to have a voice. I'm sure it also has something to do with being the child of Holocaust survivors.

Jeanne: Can you talk about that a bit?

I am the eldest of three children and we are the first generation [born] here in the United States. My father was raised in Hamburg, Germany and emigrated to Holland in 1933 where he thought he would be safe from the Nazis. But during World War II he was pulled into Westerbrok, the camp that served as a transition between Amsterdam and the death camps. He kept a diary about his experiences, one which included being released twice, hiding for a time in the same neighborhood that hid Anne Frank. My mother was the youngest of five children. Her two married sisters were interned in Bergen Belsen, but my mother was permitted to remain at home. Her sister also kept a diary, and many years later, when she earned her Ph.D., her thesis focused on diaries written in the camps. So my parents' histories taught me the value of preserving stories, the records of vital experience.

My parents emigrated to New York after the war, where I was born, and later my brother and sister. We were raised with a sensitivity to my father's need for calm, for order. If there was any arguing or dissent, we understood that had to happen before he came home at night. So even as a child I learned about the themes of illness, death, and loss.

Perhaps not surprisingly, both my sister and I turned to health care. My sister is a nurse employed in hospice type work (people with cancer, and more recently AIDS), and even early in my career I gravitated toward working with people who are aging or seriously ill. Both my sister and I find it incredibly rewarding to listen to the stories. The stories may be actual fact, or perceptions, or feelings, or even sometimes the psychotic pieces that almost give sense to an otherwise irrational person. I've learned about the history of a city or a neighborhood, the culture a person comes from, the questions they struggle to answer. I just keep listening. I find that stories define us, our culture, our community, our history, our way of thinking about the future.

Jeanne: Why are women's stories more difficult to gather? How does the experience of coping with HIV/AIDS differ when women rather than gay men have the virus?

Well, the first obvious reason is that they are women operating in our society. The virus doesn't manifest itself in the same ways in women and yet most of the medical diagnostic procedures are based on the male model. Consequently, women are often misdiagnosed, or their diagnosis is delayed. Often they are picked up at a more advanced stage in the disease.

Their social and economic positions also influence their experience with AIDS. Often they are caretakers, sometimes caring for an infected husband, sometimes bearing the sole responsibility for children. Frequently they have limited incomes, or they haven't been able to save as much as the men.

AIDS creates a stigma for all people who have it, men or women, gay or straight. But women bear a special stigma. In gay male HIV groups you rarely hear the question anymore 'how did you get it,' but women ask and are asked repeatedly, 'how did you become infected?' Sadly, those who became infected because of having sex with an HIV+ husband or partner often separate themselves from those who became infected from IV drug use. There's a much more sympathetic acceptance for the former group—or for those infected by transfusion or through the birth process—than for IV drug users, or former users.

Women are a smaller group and in this community most of the services are designed to support gay males, so often women feel isolated, invisible. Many encounter rejection from families or grief from children and family members which, as good caretakers, they try to attend to. As much as the medical world will say that illness can be treated similarly for men and women, history proves that women have to be their own advocates, they have to insist on a medical acknowledgement of what is different in their physiology in order for diagnosis and treatment to be effective.

Jeanne: In working with HIV/AIDS populations, what do you see as crucial in the next five years?

I think protease inhibitors [which arrived in the spring and summer, 1996] pose the biggest challenges. Some argue that in combination with other anti-virals the protease inhibitors will reduce AIDS to a chronic but controllable illness. Does that mean AIDS disappears from your blood stream? Does it mean that it will be available to all regardless of cost? Does it mean that people who traded in all their assets to come to Provincetown to die now face the prospect of living a long time, perhaps re-entering the work force?

Protease inhibitors are very exciting and I don't want to just talk about the negatives. But I'm scared too. I fear that these very expensive medicines could split this community into the haves and the have-nots, could delay even longer the incorporation of women and multiracial groups in the support services here. Part of what Provincetown does best is make people feel safe. What if that safety is threatened for some and not all? We may have to learn to live in community all over again.

❧

Carole

Carole holds the unenviable distinction of being the only one of our narrators to be interviewed twice. When she came forward to tell her story in the summer of 1996 she graciously offered to have us come to her home, a wonderful high-roofed chalet in the woods on the outskirts of the East End. So riveted to her story were we that we skipped the usual audio check on our tape recorder, discovering later that the high ceilings had "eaten" her low throaty voice. When we returned to Provincetown in October, she agreed to another session—this time in a small compact studio where voices could be heard clearly.

Carole's is not a voice easily muffled. Since her diagnosis three years ago, she has been an active speaker and advocate for women, appearing repeatedly in front of medical groups and health-care providers. She views the delay and dissembling surrounding her own case as not simply a personal tragedy, but an experience all too common to women, particularly white, middle class, married women not considered "at risk" for AIDS.

She also understands the agony of having to tell two daughters— one a gifted Harvard student, the other a special needs child to whom she had pledged lifelong support—that their parents have AIDS. Since no counseling was offered to Carole or her husband at the time, the process was a brutal one, an intense exchange among grieving and emotionally assaulted people who had been given no insulating gloves before incendiary material was thrust into their hands.

About a year ago, Carole and her husband left an affluent Boston suburb, sold most of their belongings and came to Provincetown, a place she believes she "was meant to be." Although she is on the Consumer Advisory Board of PASG, maintains an active speaking schedule, and works at a local art gallery, she says her life of frenetic activity is over. Now there is time to walk by the sea.

Pam: Perhaps you could begin by describing the struggle you went through before your diagnosis was made.

> Well, it started in 1990. My husband had to take me to the emergency room with terrible pelvic pain. It turned out I had pelvic inflammatory disease—one of the markers of HIV in women, I discovered later. The doctor I had was very caring and compassionate, and even though I had the sense that he

wanted to ask me more, he was reluctant. I was white, married, this was a tony suburban neighborhood hospital in Milton. You don't ask a middle-aged married woman if she's at risk for HIV. But he made sure that I got scheduled to see a highly regarded gynecologist, a woman, for a follow-up visit. When I saw her I said, "Where does something like this come from? I'm not promiscuous, I'm married. I don't understand why I have this all of a sudden." She said, "Well, don't worry about it. I'm going to write you a prescription for the new high-test antibiotic, and if you have any reoccurrences, just call me." No questions about my sex life. Nothing. I did have a couple of reoccurrences and then I started having yeast infections. Again she said, "Don't worry about it. These things happen."

In 1991 I decided to go back to school, working on a radiation therapy degree. My marriage was strained almost to the breaking point, I was losing weight, and I just kept having these intractable infections. At one point I went down to 104 pounds. I had this big ten-room house and was the stereotype overachieving, everything's-all-right Mom. I had my special needs daughter at home who requires constant care. Our older daughter was two years into Harvard, home a lot. I was trying to run on overdrive. Go to school in the day, clean the house at night. Everything exhausted me. I can remember having company over one night, standing upstairs in the den, holding onto the wall, just weaving on my feet, thinking "there's something wrong."

So I started going to doctors—about the fatigue, about the infections. In March of that year, my lymph nodes swelled up. I waited a month, they were still swollen all under my arms, on my neck. By now I was starting to get headaches, diarrhea—all the classic symptoms. I went in for my physical at school and they told me it was "nerves"; they prescribed tranquilizers. I remember clearly the doctor I saw for the school medical check. I described my full range of symptoms to him. Now this was someone attached to the hospital where I was studying, a hospital that serves a significant at-risk population. Wouldn't you think my symptoms would have screamed at him? He told me it was "nerves." Between 1990 and 1992 I saw seven or eight doctors for a variety of symptoms.

Summer came and I just kept getting worse. On the advice of a friend I went to a clinic near my house. At the time my husband's union-based insurance had lapsed, so I was relying on just school insurance. It was my first experience with clinic care. The physician I had must have performed every exotic blood test in the world (her speciality was hematology), but the only thing she could come up with was chronic fatigue syndrome. Of course by this time I was a good anatomy student, so every time she sent me to the lab I'd go back home and check in my books what she was treating me for. Lupus, toxoplasmosis, other more exotic things that would explain fatigue and malaise. Not once did she mention HIV. Not once did she ask about my marriage, my sex life or lack of sex life.

By March of '93 I had begun to have night sweats. She was writing prescriptions for Xanax constantly. So I was very well tranquilized. I remember one night I was lying in bed studying my anatomy book, looking at a section on the immune system, and I turned to my husband and said, "These look like all my symptoms. Is there any chance I could have this?" It was my way of asking, "Is there anything you need to tell me?" He laughed. I slept a little better that night. But it was still there.

Finally in June I confronted the doctor. I asked her point blank, "Do you have any idea what's wrong with me?" Clearly she didn't and reluctantly referred me to a surgeon. He examined me for five minutes, then studied me and said, "You know, I see a lot of anxiety in your eyes. Do you think this could have an emotional component?" He continued, "I just performed an operation where I removed a woman's lymph nodes—but they were just fine."

I looked at him and said, "What you see in my eyes is fear. I don't know what's wrong with me." So he agreed to biopsy the lymph nodes. Ten days later he called to say that I didn't have cancer. When I pressed him to know what the biopsy showed he said, "There's some dysplasia of the cells."

"Could you translate that please?"

"Sometimes that's an indicator of an autoimmune disorder, like rheumatoid arthritis." I kind of got dismissed.

When I called in the results to the clinic I talked with another doctor who said, "I don't mean to offend you, but is there any chance you might be at risk for HIV?" I said, "I don't follow my husband twenty-four hours a day. So let's do the test. Let's eliminate it as a possibility." Of course, he didn't do it, but referred me to another doctor, an infectious disease specialist. She never led me to believe I was in any way at risk, never recommended counseling to me, but spent the majority of the time talking about where I had traveled, what exotic places I had visited. The usual rigmarole. When she tossed off the question, "Do you want to come in or be called with the results?" She was so casual. I just said, "Call me."

Friday the 13th; I got that call. It was like a nuclear bomb exploded on my head. My daughter was in the other room. Remember this is a child, mentally retarded, who has all sorts of emotional problems, the child I promised I would always protect. She heard me screaming, "I'm going to die" and she came running in to hug me, to comfort me, to try to be there for me. [Long pause.]

I called my husband at work. He was on a job site and afterwards he told me that he seriously considered driving the car into a tree. He knew.

My husband was tested; his T-cells were 221 and mine were 311. Since he wasn't symptomatic at all I guess denial was possible for him. He didn't want to acknowledge it. Michael was really—well, I'm not sure you can imagine how he felt. At least he had a really kind social worker guiding him through the testing procedures.

Of course immediately they want to start you on drugs. You

have to take AZT, blah, blah, blah. But for women there is so little research on the effect or effectiveness of drug therapy. Here I am battling a life-threatening illness and I have no data to support any medical decisions that I make. There is absolutely no research on women. There *still* isn't.

I felt we had to tell our daughter—the older one. I didn't tell the younger one because her therapist thought this was not information she could process. Of course after that scene on the phone she knew something was terribly wrong. But we told the older daughter two weeks after our diagnosis. We had no counseling; we were still angry, still grieving. I realize it was a big mistake. It was a terrible, terrible scene. We all said some unforgivable things to each other because we were not in a place where we could talk about it reasonably. We were all too raw. She ended up leaving after a terrible fight. And we weren't reunited until right before I came down to Provincetown.

Jeanne: How did you begin your public speaking work?

I saw an acupuncturist in Brookline who was treating me for neuropathy and who was part of the AIDS CARE project at that time. He said, "There's a course you should look into that Anne Webster runs at Deaconess, part of the mind–body course. It's wonderful." So I went and enrolled. That really kept me going. It taught me that to survive I needed to develop a spiritual core, a connection to something larger than self. I loved that class; twenty gay men and me.

AIDS Awareness Day rolled around December 1, 1993, and in class that evening Anne went around the circle and asked us to speak about our feelings. Of course, many of the men felt anger, felt grief, had lived with this much longer than I. When she turned to me and I started talking I remember saying, "You know, respectfully, I haven't lived with this as long as you have and I haven't suffered the losses you have, but you have to understand that I don't feel that this is just a gay man's disease anymore. If this can happen to me, just think what it's like for women who don't have the resources I do, or don't have the education." That's really the first time I spoke up and people came up later to tell me that they had never thought through the implications of the issues I was raising, that I ought to speak publicly about it.

So I started speaking—initially to groups of doctors. It was really a catharsis, a way of healing some of the hurt and anger and betrayal I felt at the medical establishment. I think I've changed a few people's opinions. I hope so. I continue to speak both about my story and about the need for research on women.

My husband left his job that January and he went to bed. He didn't get up for three months. I couldn't get him into therapy; I was lucky if I could get him to see his doctor. And people asked me then and even now why I didn't leave him.

You know, he didn't set out to make me sick. And I couldn't see how we were better off apart. It didn't make sense to me. If ever there was a time we needed each other it was then. I loved him. I loved him. [Long pause.]

But once I opened my mouth and started speaking, started asserting myself, I knew I had to change my life in profound ways. I looked around Boston and decided that my big ten-room house represented everything that was wrong with who I was. I had volunteered to do a fund-raiser in Provincetown in August, and on the spur of the moment, I rented a cottage here and said to my husband, "Why don't you come down, too? You'll really like it." I remember walking on the beach and thinking, now I understand how you connect the spiritual part of what's inside you with what's outside you. Not only is it physically beautiful, but there's a quality of respectfulness in the community. When you get HIV you recognize an HIV community, and I glimpsed it on the street. But both my husband and I felt more in tune with things that we ever had before in our lives. On the last day I remember turning to my husband as we walked down the street and saying, "How would you like to live here?" He said, "Do you mean it?" And we both knew we did mean it.

Things just fell into place. The woman I rented the cottage from was a realtor who knew a realtor in Boston who helped me sell the big house. Then we located the place here. It was like somebody drew an arrow in the sky.

Pam: Do you feel that as a woman there are any barriers to hurdle at PASG where almost all the clients are gay men?

Well, I've broken a lot of barriers since I've had this disease. My husband and I started almost immediately going to the dinners, making friends. I'm accustomed to making friends with gay men. After all, when most of my Boston friends deserted me it was the gay men who offered support. Who else to better understand what you're going through? At first I think we turned a few heads when we attended the dinners, but I never allowed myself to feel that we didn't belong there. My case manager suggested that I go to a Consumer Advisory Board meeting. So I did and now I'm on the Board. I found that people were glad that I was there. Ginnine [Principe] came up one day and said exactly that, "Oh, I've been praying for a woman to come. I'm so glad you're here." My husband volunteered at the PASG auction and drives the van to Boston.

Most recently I've completed a peer education training program through Positive Directions. It's a program out of Boston designed for people who are living with AIDS to educate and help others living with AIDS. It's especially effective for women since the great majority of them are taking care of another sick person, or children.

You know it may sound corny but I think I was meant to be here—to be a part of that bridge between men and women living with AIDS as we move toward the twenty-first century. To help with the understanding that this disease has no boundaries. I think I was meant to take one or two steps toward creating that bridge. What else matters as much?

❧

Wendy

Wendy knows Provincetown from the inside out. Sent to live with an uncle at the age of twelve, she has lived year-round in the village for the past twenty years. During that period of time she's witnessed the economic decline of the fishing industry, the real estate boom of the '80s, and the invasion of AIDS into every corner of the community.

For eight years Wendy cared for her husband, who died of AIDS in January of this year. Only recently has she turned her attention to her own HIV+ diagnosis and health care. Dark-haired, vivacious, with a quick laugh, she looks much younger than her years and experience might suggest. She generously agreed to be interviewed early one October Saturday morning, even though she had worked until 1 A.M. the previous evening.

Pam: You've been in Provincetown for a number of years now. How did that come about?

I came down to live with my "uncles" when I was twelve. Actually it was my uncle and his lover, but I didn't realize they were gay at the time. I just called them both my uncles. It was a good move for me. At home I had a large family: three sisters and two brothers. And I was getting to be too much for my mother to handle. Here In Provincetown I learned a lot. I learned how to be open, avoid prejudice, grow. The rest of my family, brothers and sisters that is, are really homophobic. They wouldn't even attend my wedding because the best man, my friend, was gay.

Provincetown is beautiful. People are there to support you, straight or gay. There is nothing to fear here. That made it much easier when Steve, my husband, got sick. Only recently I've gone back to Plymouth—I guess because I was seeing so much death. But when I get there I want to go back home to

Provincetown. The same thing that kicks me out brings me back. It's the understanding. The understanding. If you're HIV+ like I am, you don't have to be afraid—to use the toilet, to drink frrom a neighbor's cup. If I go over to Ethel's—my eighty-six-year-old neighbor—she knows I'm positive and she doesn't care. "Here you are," she says. If I go to Plymouth, it's a very different thing.

Pam: When did you get married?

I got married in 1988. We got tested before we got married, both of us tested negative, and six months later, after we were married, Steve tested positive.

Pam: Why did you get tested a second time?

Because we decided to have children. We needed to change a medical policy for added benefits, and in the course of that, they did blood tests. They called us and simply said, "Go to your doctor." We had no idea what it could be. Of course we had no pre-test counseling or anything like that, since we were negative six months earlier.

You have to realize that in the past Steve had been a drug user. But I also knew he had been clean for five years and passed our pre-marriage blood test. So we figured we were safe.

It's ironic really because living in Provincetown I knew all about HIV. I was well informed. I took special care not to date bisexual men. Even in the mid-'80s when it was still thought of as a gay disease, I was very careful. Of course I knew that IV drug use put somebody at risk. So that's why I insisted on the blood tests. Now I realize that Steve's first test must have been misread, because when he tested positive six months later his numbers were very, very low. He must have been positive a long time.

The news was very hard for Steve to handle. He grew depressed. He just couldn't accept the fact that he infected me. As the months went on he turned it around on me, saying I infected him. I went through a lot of emotional abuse during his illness.

Pam: How did you deal with taking care of him and dealing with your own health?

I didn't take care of my health. He took full time care and attention. He had dementia, he went blind. I was the mother and he was the child. I had to handle it for him.

I really don't know why it didn't take a bigger toll on my health. Because when I was first diagnosed doctors said, this was 1988, "You're a woman; you'll be dead in four months."

After Steve was gone—my husband passed away in January of this year—it was hard for me to go on, to find a purpose. I've talked with Irene [Cramer] a lot about this, about discovering what I want to do, where I want to go from here, but after years of worrying about, caring for Steve, it's hard for me to focus on my future.

Still, this virus has taught me so much. Like who your real friends are. Like what employers will duck when you reveal your HIV status. In Provincetown you can interview for a job with anybody and reveal your HIV+ status. But in Plymouth, forget it. I've learned who in my family I can talk to and who I can't, whose kids I can touch and whose I can't. And I've learned—rather, I'm learning, how to watch over my own medical records, the history of my own medications, ask questions of the doctors.

Jeanne: I gather your family hasn't been entirely supportive.

My mom and dad are great; they're wonderful. My sisters are another story. One is okay. But the two others don't allow me to touch their children. My brothers don't feel that way. When they visit, they almost throw the kids into my arms. But one of my sisters said, for example, "Well, you can come over to the house, but be careful not to get any saliva in the cups." What does she think I'm going to do? Drool? Spit in all her cups? [Laughter.]

I knew when I moved back into my parents' house for a while this year that those sisters wouldn't visit because I was there. My mom used to see those kids every day, so I warned her, "You know, you're not going to see your grandchildren anymore because I'm here." And she hasn't.

Pam: Have you had support from PASG?

The Provincetown AIDS Support Group was there for me when Steve was dying. They tried to do everything they could for me. But it's a group that is built on men and for men. When I went in there to have dinner after Steve passed away, I got looks from folks. Finally somebody came over and asked, "What are you doing here?" So I had to say, "I'm a client too."

And after Steve died I heard about a grieving group at PASG, a group that helps you learn to handle the loss. A friend said, "Why don't you join?", but when I went to sign up I was told it was closed to me; it was for men only. Finally I got Carole to go to some things with me. Both of us got on the Consumer Advisory Board, but I dropped out. It's hard for me to listen to negativity, maybe because my husband's reaction to the virus was all negativity. As soon as he found out he was HIV+ he was dying with the virus, he wasn't living with the virus.

I think the way PASG operates makes people associate the virus with a "gay disease." They have men in drag out on the streets passing out condoms, for example. You never see a woman out there, or a straight man. In fact I have people come up to me, people who don't know that I'm HIV+, and who whisper, "I can tell anybody who has the virus. I can just pick them out." "Oh, yeah?" I say. [Laughter.]

I've had other kinds of support here, however. It's physically beautiful here. I never tire of sitting by the water watching the sun set. The openness in the whole town is a spiritual thing too.

And I go to St. Peter's where the priest and the people of

that church have been just wonderful to me. A lot of people don't think of the Catholic Church as being very open, but the church serves this community, its needs, and many in the community are gay. They're starting up an AIDS ministry now, and they do healing services. I cook at St. Peter's every Tuesday night and once a month at the AIDS Support Group.

I remember that after Steve died and was cremated people warned me that perhaps I wouldn't be allowed to bring his ashes into the church. I was scared. It was very important to me. And I think Father John must have sensed that because he said, "Get those ashes in here." [Laughter.]

Sometimes I wish that there were more women coming forward, but I also know how hard it is to be an HIV+ woman and be out in the open. Some women are taking care of husbands. Some have to protect their children. If I had a child I don't know how I'd react. It would depend on the child.

There's a lot of excitement recently about the protease inhibitors. Actually my doctors suggested that I go on them, but I'm waiting. It's complicated—just exactly when you take them— and if you mistime things, or if you miss one sequence, the virus can attack. I'm doing really well right now; my T-cell count is 375 and my viral load is really low, so I'm waiting a little. I'll have more blood work done and then try to figure it out.

You know in some ways the new drugs seem like another major shift, and already I've had so many. What I first intended to do was marry and have children. Then people say you have to come to terms with the fact that you're going to die in four months, then in five, maybe ten years. Shift. Then people say you have to come to terms with the fact that you may be living with this virus for sixty years. I'm really happy for the new medications because they will save so many lives. But they also offer such a different future than most of us thought we faced that they are also upsetting, scary really. It changes your whole outlook. How do you think about the future?

⟡

Living with HIV, as Wendy attests, requires constant accommodations, constant adjustments, constant alterations in assessing the future. But nothing in Provincetown's fourteen-year experience with AIDS has the potential to reconfigure the future more dramatically than the arrival of protease inhibitors.

On October 3, 1996, the *Wall Street Journal* ran a lengthy article entitled "Life After Death: Well Accustomed to Loss, Massachusetts Village Faces Realities of Survival." The article—which angered many in town who took issue with the ways Provincetown was characterized—discusses protease inhibitors, "the new class of drugs which, when used in combination with a set of older antiviral medicines, raises the remarkable hope of reducing AIDS to a chronic but controllable illness like diabetes, as opposed to a likely death sentence within ten years." A variety of health care givers and HIV+ residents are quoted in the article, among them Dr. Len Alberts, Douglas Brooks, and Len Stewart of PASG. Each expresses the elation and confusion that accompanies the seemingly miraculous arrival of the new medications. Public awareness of the results of new drug combinations dates only from the International AIDS Conference in Vancouver in June of 1996. In early November, the third International Congress on Drug Therapy held in Birmingham, England reported research which indicated an almost complete suppression of HIV infection in patients treated with protease inhibitors (saquinavir and two types of ritonavir).

While people in Provincetown view the data as potentially very exciting, it is still too early to be anything but cautiously optimistic. Some patients have experienced adverse side effects like diarrhea, fatigue, and nausea, so for those already seriously compromised by AIDS, protease inhibitors may not be an option. The high cost of the drugs may also polarize a community that has worked hard to create a level playing field for all infected by the virus. For those who stand to gain increased health and mobility from the new medication, the picture is also complicated. Some sold their assets and moved to Provincetown with the expectation that they would die within eight or ten years.

Now faced with the prospect of a "manageable chronic disease," they may need to re-enter a workforce they left a decade ago. Since Provincetown already suffers from an unemployment problem, they'll have to look for jobs elsewhere.

At the close of 1996, change is in the air, as palpable as the onset of snow. With history's eerie echoing, the navigational challenges Provincetown faces at the close of the twentieth century are as formidable as those it faced at the beginning of the century.

Cape Codders have been rescuing their rescue stations, saving their life-saving lights, for two decades now. During the summer of 1996 the oldest lighthouse on the Cape, the Highland Light, was painstakingly jacked up and moved 450 feet back from the pounding Atlantic surf that had eroded its shore. Often referred to as the "Cape Cod Light," the original lighthouse was constructed in 1787 in North Truro and rebuilt in 1857. Thoreau enjoyed the hospitality of the keeper's house on his travels to Provincetown, and the light not only illuminated the dangerous shoals that Champlain called Cap Mallebarre ("Cape Evil Bars"), it also served as a navigational aid orienting ships into Provincetown Harbor. Moving the multi-ton sixty-six-foot-high lighthouse took months of planning and years of fundraising. But in July the lighthouse was eased on to steel track beams; it inched along tracks lubricated with Ivory Soap, cheered on by hundreds of witnesses. Down Cape, Nauset Light poses the next challenge; the beloved red-and-white landmark currently stands just forty-five feet from the Atlantic surf, and officials are planning its move in the coming year. In October, about the time the *Wall Street Journal* wrote its troubling article, Highland Light was reactivated.

What accounts for this prodigious effort to save lighthouses and rescue stations from certain destruction? What fuels the desire to preserve picturesque but nonessential relics of the past? Modern navigational techniques render lighthouses unnecessary—and yet one on-looker, who observed Highland Light's snail-like progress to its new location, was moved to exclaim, "It's not dramatic, but it's a beautiful thing."

Beyond the value of historic preservation, beyond the creation of yet another "tourist spot," the Cape's lighthouses and life-saving stations stand in mute testimony to human ingenuity in the face of danger. Their unique "beauty" lies in their symbolism, for they remind us of the whole spectrum of human response to danger: warning, illumination, vigilance, rescue, survival, loss, grief, comfort.

Race Point, a spot where almost insurmountable risk collided with the human determination to surmount it, speaks not only with voices from its past. It is the look-out point, alive with voices of the present. Listen:

> "A devastating disease was heading our way, one that was going to be affecting our friends and neighbors. Provincetown was medically isolated, and a system of health and home care services needed to be put into place. In the meantime, it was a question of educating the community, of combatting fear, of learning as much about the disease as we could."

> "At first even the medical people were terrified; they wore masks, gloves, hats—they looked like astronauts. But many people too were guided by what was in their hearts."

> "I suppose a crisis will either elevate people or not. A lot of people have allowed the AIDS crisis to elevate them physically and spiritually ... Maybe they've always wanted to write, so they write. Maybe they've always wanted to paint, so they paint. They decide to extract everything they can out of life."

> "I don't think disease can create, but rather it defines what was already there—intensifies it."

> "See that little spit of land? That is Cape Cod and right at its tip is Provincetown. There's something special here: the light,

color, air, the people. The *people*. Even at 30,000 feet this community looks good."

"If you look at the whole spectrum of women's health issues, HIV will be at the bottom of the list. There's shame attached to a sexually transmitted or drug-related disease. It's a stage that will pass. Remember when we were kids everybody whispered the word *cancer*."

"I find that stories define us, our culture, our community, our history, our way of thinking about the future. I just keep listening."

"Provincetown is both an edge and a gateway. Many of us who have made this place our home have done so because we have felt ourselves on the margins in other places, and that experience in itself has been a gateway to learning and growth."

January 1996–December 1996. The wheel of the seasons turns. Once again winter skies accompany our journeys back and forth to town, out on the Breakwater, out the fire road to Hatches Harbor, up to the wind-swept expanses of Race Point Beach. On winter nights when the dark sky is cloudless, Orion dominates the constellations, the Hunter outlined in bright stars. Using the three stars of Orion's belt, the Bull and the Pleiades emerge. And, pointing backward, Sirius glows, Orion's dog star, the brightest star in the heavens. The Big and Little Dipper, easily recognizable all year, stand out as if immersed in the acid bath of a daguerreotype.

Like other big sky places—Montana, the Dakotas, the deserts of Arizona and New Mexico—the stars in Provincetown need not compete with big city neon or industrial illuminations. Set against the dark sea and snow covered sand they shine with elemental brilliance, or sometimes with the kind of cascading showers of light that New

Englanders associate with the Boston Pops' rendition of the "1812 Overture." No timpani, cannon, Roman candles imploding here, however. Space. Silence. The magnetic lap of the waves. The skin of solitude.

Are stars the gates to understanding our own loneliness and longing?

Astronomers say that all matter that composes our planet was hurled into the cosmos at once. Or, as Carl Sagan has remarked, "we are all made of star stuff." In Provincetown, more easily than most places, it is possible to feel affinity with the stars.

Perhaps that is why the Provincetown AIDS Support Group's panel, the one displayed with the AIDS quilt, portrays this quotation from *Romeo and Juliet* (Act III, scene ii) and the names of residents who have died of AIDS stitched into stars.

> *... and when he shall die,*
> *Take him and cut him out in little stars*
> *And he will make the face of heaven so fine*
> *That all the world will be in love with night*
> *And pay no worship to the garish sun.*

A description of the quilt and its star motif reached us six months into the writing of this narrative, long after we had chosen our title. When a receptionist at PASG showed us a photo of the AIDS panel and congratulated us on the appropriateness of the book's title, we reacted with an involuntary shudder—as if the birds had just flown over Delphi. It was a moment of eerie synchronicity—one impossible to examine with the cold eye of logic.

To walk in Provincetown in the winter is to be in touch not only with the starry, starry night, but also with the small insistent lamps burning in the store fronts, in dormered cottages, high in second story studios. How incandescent it must have seemed when streets and homes were gas lighted, or earlier yet were illumined by whale oil derived from the sperm whales hunted off Stellwagon Banks. Whale oil, according to Melville, produced a "sweet lunar light, the very food of light" ("The Lamp," *Moby Dick*). It's not difficult to imagine that softer effulgence bracketing the streets, snaking out into the traceries of mews and alleyway, casting flickering auras and faintly colored arcs, more generous bodied, livelier than hard-edged electricity.

Now it is full night, clear, moonless, the enormous canopy of the sky filled with stars. The lamps are lighted, keeping faith with the sky: the running lights on boats in the harbor, the holiday lights on the Pilgrim Monument, the lighted tower of the Universalist Meeting House, the cupped candles from the Vigil, the memorial fires burning in Herring Cove, the steady beams of Race Point, Wood End, Long Point. On this little spit of land "the very food of light" burns, one long luminescent thread stitching the dark.

About the Authors

Jeanne Braham received her Bachelor of Arts degree from the College of Wooster, her Master of Arts degree from the University of Pennsylvania, and her Doctor of Arts from Carnegie-Mellon University. The author of previous books on Saul Bellow and on women's autobiography, she teaches literature and creative writing at Clark University in Massachusetts.

Pamela Peterson received her Bachelor of Arts degree from Smith College (where she was an Ada Comstock scholar) and her Master of Social Work degree from the Smith School for Social Work. A clinical social worker, she works as a counselor and advocate for the New England Learning Center for Women in Transition in Massachusetts.